I0439635

Informing the legislative debate since 1914

Wartime Detention Provisions in Recent Defense Authorization Legislation

Jennifer K. Elsea
Legislative Attorney

Michael John Garcia
Legislative Attorney

June 23, 2014

Congressional Research Service

7-5700

www.crs.gov

R42143

Summary

In recent years, Congress has included provisions in annual defense authorization bills addressing issues related to detainees at the U.S. Naval Station at Guantanamo Bay, Cuba, and, more broadly, the disposition of persons captured in the course of hostilities against Al Qaeda and associated forces. The National Defense Authorization Act for FY2012 (2012 NDAA; P.L. 112-81) arguably constituted the most significant legislation informing wartime detention policy since the 2001 Authorization for the Use of Military Force (AUMF; P.L. 107-40), which serves as the primary legal authority for U.S. operations against Al Qaeda and associated forces. Much of the debate surrounding passage of the 2012 NDAA centered on what appeared to be an effort to confirm or, as some observers view it, expand the detention authority that Congress implicitly granted the President via the AUMF in the aftermath of the terrorist attacks of September 11, 2001. But the 2012 NDAA addressed other issues as well, including the continued detention of persons at Guantanamo. Both the 2013 NDAA (P.L. 112-239) and the 2014 NDAA (P.L. 113-66) also contain subtitles addressing U.S. detention policy, though neither act addresses detention matters as comprehensively as did the 2012 NDAA. The competing House and Senate defense authorization bills for FY2015 (H.R. 4435 and S. 2410) also contain provisions addressing the continued detention of Guantanamo detainees.

The 2012 NDAA authorizes the detention of certain categories of persons and requires the military detention of a subset of them (subject to waiver); regulates status determinations for persons held pursuant to the AUMF; regulates periodic review proceedings concerning Guantanamo detainees; and continued funding restrictions on Guantanamo detainee transfers. During floor debate, significant attention centered on the extent to which the bill and existing law permit the military detention of U.S. citizens believed to be enemy belligerents, especially if arrested within the United States. The enacted version included a provision clarifying that the act's affirmation of detention authority under the AUMF is not intended to affect existing authorities relating to the detention of U.S. citizens or lawful resident aliens, or any other persons arrested in the United States. When signing the 2012 NDAA into law, President Obama stated that he would "not authorize the indefinite military detention without trial of American citizens."

The 2012 NDAA and subsequent defense authorization enactments also included provisions concerning the transfer or release of detainees currently held at Guantanamo. Both the 2012 and 2013 NDAAs extended the existing prohibition on the release of detainees into the United States for any purpose, as well as restrictions upon the transfer of such Guantanamo detainees to foreign countries. The 2014 NDAA extends the blanket prohibition on transferring Guantanamo detainees to the United States, but allows the Executive greater flexibility in determining whether to transfer detainees to foreign custody. The competing House and Senate defense authorization bills for FY2015 take different approaches toward Guantanamo detention policy. Whereas H.R. 4435, as passed by the House, would maintain current restrictions, S. 2410, as reported by the Senate Armed Services Committee, would establish a process by which the Executive could potentially transfer Guantanamo detainees into the country for continued detention or trial.

This report offers a brief background of the salient issues raised by the detainee provisions of the FY2012 NDAA, provides a section-by-section analysis, and discusses executive interpretation and implementation of the act's mandatory military detention provision. It also addresses detainee provisions in the 2013 NDAA and 2014 NDAA, as well as those found in the competing House and Senate defense authorization bills for FY2015. An earlier version of this report was entitled *The National Defense Authorization Act for FY2012 and Beyond: Detainee Matters*.

Contents

Contacts

In recent years, Congress has included provisions in annual defense authorization bills addressing issues related to detainees at the U.S. Naval Station at Guantanamo Bay, Cuba, and, more broadly, the disposition of persons captured in the course of hostilities against Al Qaeda and associated forces. The National Defense Authorization Act for FY2012 (2012 NDAA; P.L. 112-81) arguably constituted the most significant legislation informing wartime detention policy since the 2001 Authorization for the Use of Military Force (AUMF; P.L. 107-40), which serves as the primary legal authority for U.S. operations against Al Qaeda and associated forces. Both the National Defense Authorization Acts for FY2013 (2013 NDAA; P.L. 112-239) and FY2014 (2014 NDAA; P.L. 113-66) contain subtitles addressing U.S. detention policy, particularly with respect to persons held at Guantanamo, though neither act addresses detention matters as comprehensively as the 2012 NDAA.

The 2012 NDAA authorizes the detention of certain categories of persons and requires the military detention of a subset of them; regulates status determinations for persons held pursuant to the AUMF; regulates periodic review proceedings concerning the continued detention of Guantanamo detainees; and continued funding restrictions that relate to Guantanamo detainee transfers to foreign countries (funding restrictions that were subsequently loosened by the 2014 NDAA). The 2012 NDAA continued the bar on the use of Department of Defense (DOD) funds to transfer detainees from Guantanamo into the United States for trial or other purposes (a bar that Congress has extended through subsequent appropriations and defense authorization enactments), and although it does not directly bar criminal trials for terrorism suspects, it requires the Attorney General to consult with the Defense Department and Director of National Intelligence prior to bringing charges or seeking an indictment in certain cases. The act also contains (1) a modified provision from the House bill that requires a report to Congress detailing the "national security protocol" pertaining to the communications of persons detained at Guantanamo, (2) a requirement for quarterly briefings on counterterrorism operations, and (3) a requirement for the President to issue national security guidelines for denying safe havens to Al Qaeda and its affiliates in countries that may be vulnerable. Further, the act makes some modifications to the Military Commissions Act (MCA).[1]

During congressional deliberations over the House and Senate bills, the White House criticized each version's detainee provisions, and threatened to veto any legislation "that challenges or constrains the President's critical authorities to collect intelligence, incapacitate dangerous terrorists, and protect the Nation."[2] In particular, the Administration expressed strong opposition to any provision mandating the military detention of certain categories of persons, limiting executive discretion as to the appropriate forum to prosecute terrorist suspects, or constraining the executive's ability to transfer detainees from U.S. custody.

The version of the 2012 NDAA passed by Congress included a few modifications intended to assuage some of the Administration's concerns. The conference report dropped a House provision that would have required military commissions for certain terrorism cases and modified the House provision prohibiting the transfer of terrorism suspects to the United States for trial so that it only applies to those held at Guantanamo and not to all suspects detained abroad. It modified

---

[1] Chapter 47a of Title 10, *U.S. Code.*

[2] *See* Exec. Office of the Pres., Statement of Administration Policy on H.R. 1540 (May 24, 2011) (hereinafter "White House Statement on H.R. 1540"), *available at* http://www.whitehouse.gov/sites/default/files/omb/legislative/sap/112/saphr1540r_20110524.pdf; Exec. Office of the Pres., Statement of Administration Policy on S. 1867 (November 17, 2011) (hereinafter "White House Statement on S. 1867"), *available at* http://www.whitehouse.gov/sites/default/files/omb/legislative/sap/112/saps1867s_20111117.pdf.

the Senate provision mandating the military detention of certain categories of persons (originally subject to waiver by the Secretary of Defense) by adding a statement to that provision to confirm that it does not affect "the existing criminal enforcement and national security authorities of the Federal Bureau of Investigation or any other domestic law enforcement agency," even with respect to persons held in military custody. The conferees also transferred the waiver authority from the Secretary of Defense to the President. The conference report retained language added during Senate floor debate to clarify that the provision affirming the authority to detain persons captured in the conflict with Al Qaeda does not modify any existing authorities relating to the power to detain U.S. citizens or lawful resident aliens, or any other persons captured or arrested in the United States.

The Obama Administration then lifted its veto threat,[3] and President Obama signed the 2012 NDAA into law on December 31, 2011. Nonetheless, President Obama issued a signing statement criticizing many of the act's detainee provisions, in which he pledged to interpret certain provisions in a manner that would preserve a maximum degree of flexibility and discretion in the handling of captured terrorists.[4] Among other things, he criticized the blanket bar on Guantanamo detainee transfers into the United States and the restrictions imposed on detainee transfers to foreign countries, arguing that some applications of these provisions might violate constitutional separation of powers principles. President Obama also announced that he would "not authorize the indefinite military detention without trial of American citizens," regardless of whether such detention might be legally permissible under the AUMF or the 2012 NDAA. He further declared that his Administration would not "adhere to a rigid across-the-board requirement for military detention," and suggested that he would exercise the statutory waiver of the mandatory military detention provision when he deemed it appropriate. On February 28, 2012, President Obama issued a directive describing circumstances in which the 2012 NDAA's mandatory military detention requirement would be waived.[5]

Both the 2013 and 2014 versions of the NDAA contain subtitles addressing U.S. detention policy, particularly with respect to persons held at Guantanamo. While the detention provisions in the 2013 NDAA largely represented a continuation of existing policies, the 2014 NDAA saw some relaxation of the long-standing restrictions imposed upon the transfer of Guantanamo detainees to foreign countries.

This report offers a brief background of the salient issues and provides a section-by-section analysis of the detainee provisions in the National Defense Authorization Act for FY2012. It also discusses executive interpretation and implementation of the act's mandatory military detention provision. Finally, it addresses detainee provisions in the 2013 NDAA and the 2014 NDAA, as well as the detainee provisions found in the House and Senate defense authorization bills for FY2015.

---

[3] *See* Charlie Savage, *Obama Drops Veto Threat Over Military Authorization Bill After Revisions*, N.Y. TIMES, December 14, 2011, at A30, *available at* http://www.nytimes.com/2011/12/15/us/politics/obama-wont-veto-military-authorization-bill html?_r=3.

[4] White House, Office of the Press Secretary, Statement by the President on H.R. 1540, December 31, 2011 (hereinafter "Presidential Signing Statement on 2012 NDAA"), *available at* http://www.whitehouse.gov/the-press-office/2011/12/31/statement-president-hr-1540.

[5] Presidential Policy Directive, Procedures Implementing Section 1022 of the National Defense Authorization Act for Fiscal Year (FY) 2012, February 28, 2012 (hereinafter "Presidential Policy Directive on Section 1022"), *available at* http://www.justice.gov/opa/documents/ppd-14.pdf.

Background

At the heart of the consideration of the detainee provisions in the 2012 NDAA appears to have been an effort to confirm or, as some observers view it, expand the detention authority Congress implicitly granted the President in the aftermath of the terrorist attacks of September 11, 2001. In enacting the Authorization for Use of Military Force (AUMF; P.L. 107-40), Congress authorized the President

> to use all necessary and appropriate force against those nations, organizations, or persons he determines planned, authorized, committed, or aided the terrorist attacks that occurred on September 11, 2001, or harbored such organizations or persons, in order to prevent any future acts of international terrorism against the United States by such nations, organizations or persons.

Many persons captured during subsequent U.S operations in Afghanistan and elsewhere have been placed in preventive detention to stop them from participating in hostilities or terrorist activities. A few have been tried by military commission for crimes associated with those hostilities,[6] while many others have been tried for terrorism-related crimes in civilian court.

In the 2004 case of *Hamdi v. Rumsfeld*, a majority of the Supreme Court recognized that, as a necessary incident to the AUMF, the President may detain enemy combatants captured while fighting U.S. forces in Afghanistan (including U.S. citizens), and potentially hold such persons for the duration of hostilities.[7] The *Hamdi* decision left to lower courts the task of defining the scope of detention authority conferred by the AUMF, including whether the authorization permits the detention of members or supporters of Al Qaeda, the Taliban, or other groups who are apprehended away from the Afghan zone of combat.

Most subsequent judicial activity concerning U.S. detention policy has occurred in the D.C. Circuit, where courts have considered numerous habeas petitions by Guantanamo detainees challenging the legality of their detention. Rulings by the U.S. Court of Appeals for the D.C. Circuit have generally been favorable to the legal position advanced by the government regarding the scope of its detention authority under the AUMF.[8] It remains to be seen whether any of these rulings will be reviewed by the Supreme Court and, if such review occurs, whether the Court will endorse or reject the circuit court's understanding of the AUMF and the scope of detention authority it confers.

---

[6] To date there have been six convictions by military commissions, four of which were procured by plea agreement, and two additional guilty pleas have been entered. One conviction has been reversed on appeal, and another appeal is scheduled for rehearing en banc at the U.S. Court of Appeals for the D.C. Circuit. Two new appeals have been filed at the Court of Military Commissions Review. The current status of military commissions can be found at http://www.mc.mil/CASES/MilitaryCommissions.aspx. For more information about military commissions, see CRS Report R40932, *Comparison of Rights in Military Commission Trials and Trials in Federal Criminal Court*, by Jennifer K. Elsea.

[7] Hamdi v. Rumsfeld, 542 U.S. 507, 518 (2004) (O'Connor, J., plurality opinion); *id.* at 588-589 (Thomas, J., dissenting).For more information about relevant court decisions, see CRS Report R41156, *Judicial Activity Concerning Enemy Combatant Detainees: Major Court Rulings*, by Jennifer K. Elsea and Michael John Garcia.

[8] *See* CRS Report R41156, *Judicial Activity Concerning Enemy Combatant Detainees: Major Court Rulings*, by Jennifer K. Elsea and Michael John Garcia.

Prior to the 2012 NDAA, Congress did not pass any legislation to directly assist the courts in defining the scope of detention authority granted by the AUMF. The D.C. Circuit has, however, looked to other post-AUMF legislation concerning the jurisdiction of military commissions for guidance as to the categories of persons who may be subject to military detention. In 2010, the circuit court concluded that the government had authority under the AUMF to detain militarily persons subject to the jurisdiction of military commissions established pursuant to the Military Commissions Acts of 2006 and 2009 (MCA); namely, those who are "part of forces associated with Al Qaeda or the Taliban," along with "those who purposefully and materially support such forces in hostilities against U.S. Coalition partners."[9]

Most of the persons detained under the authority of the AUMF are combatants picked up during military operations in Afghanistan or arrested elsewhere abroad. Many of these individuals were transported to the U.S. Naval Station at Guantanamo Bay, Cuba, for detention in military custody, although a few "high value" Guantanamo detainees were initially held at other locations by the CIA for interrogation. The United States held a larger number of detainees at a facility in Parwan, Afghanistan, most of whom were captured in Afghanistan and are Afghan nationals.[10] The United States agreed to hand over control of the facility to the Afghan government, and transfer all Afghan detainees in its custody at Parwan to the Afghan authorities by September 2012,[11] though implementation of this agreement was delayed due to disagreement between Afghan and U.S.

---

[9] Al-Bihani v. Obama, 590 F.3d 866, 872 (D.C. Cir. 2010) (quoting the Military Commissions Act of 2006, P.L. 109-366, §3, and the Military Commissions Act of 2009, P.L. 111-84, Div A, §1802), *cert. denied*, 131 S. Ct. 1814 (2011). The Military Commissions Act confers jurisdiction over alien enemy unprivileged belligerents, 10 U.S.C. §948C, defining as an unprivileged belligerent a person who is not entitled to prisoner of war status under the Geneva Conventions who

> (A) has engaged in hostilities against the United States or its coalition partners;
>
> (B) has purposefully and materially supported hostilities against the United States or its coalition partners; or
>
> (C) was a part of al Qaeda at the time of the alleged offense under [chapter 47a of Title 10, *U.S. Code*].

10 U.S.C. §948A(7). Although the jurisdiction of military commissions extends only to non-citizens, the D.C. Circuit would probably include U.S. citizens who meet the definition of enemy unprivileged belligerent in its interpretation of the scope of detention authority under the AUMF, given that the *Hamdi* opinion already establishes detention authority with respect to U.S. citizens.

[10] The Parwan detention facility took over detention operations previously conducted at the Bagram Theater Internment Facility. *See* Lisa Daniel, *Task Force Ensures Fair Detainee Treatment, Commander Says*, American Forces Press Service, August 6, 2010, *available at* http://www.defense.gov/News/NewsArticle.aspx?ID=103004. The detention center had been slated to be turned over to Afghan authority by January, 2012, but rapid growth of the prisoner population caused the transfer to be delayed. *See* Kevin Sieff, *Afghan prison transfer delayed*, WASH. POST, August 12, 2011, at http://www.washingtonpost.com/world/asia-pacific/afghan-prison-transfer-delayed/2011/08/12/gIQApCGMBJ_story.html. A memorandum of understanding was entered with the Afghan government concerning the handover of the facility in March 2012. The memorandum also contemplates U.S. forces maintaining continued control of Parwan detainees during a six-month handover period, at which point all Afghan nationals in U.S. custody shall be transferred to the control of Afghanistan. Memorandum of Understanding between the Islamic Republic of Afghanistan and the United States of America on Transfer of U.S. Detention Facilities in Afghan Territory to Afghanistan, *available at* http://www.lawfareblog.com/wp-content/uploads/2012/04/2012-03-09-Signed-MOU-on-Detentions-Transfer-2.pdf [hereinafter "MOU on Parwan Transfer"]. A separate memorandum of understanding dealing with special operations in Afghanistan provides for Afghan authorities to conduct the "temporary holding" of persons detained in connection with special operations (night raids). Memorandum of Understanding between the Islamic Republic of Afghanistan and the United States of America on Afghanization of Special Operations on Afghan Soil (April 8, 2012), *available at* http://www.isaf.nato.int/images/20120408_01_memo.pdf. Afghan citizens detained by U.S. forces outside of special operations are to be transferred to Afghan authorities or released, *id.* at para. 9.

[11] MOU on Parwan Transfer, *supra* footnote 10, at para. 6.

authorities, with Afghan officials reportedly claiming that the United States continued to hold several dozen Afghan detainees.[12] The remaining Afghan prisoners were turned over to Afghanistan in March 2013 after an agreement was reached whereby U.S. advisors are to remain at the facility and Afghanistan agreed not to release prisoners the United States considers particularly dangerous.[13] Several dozen non-Afghan detainees remain in U.S. custody.[14] Neither the Guantanamo nor the Parwan facility appears to be considered a viable option for future captures that take place outside of Afghanistan; the current practice in such cases seems to be ad hoc.[15]

In almost all instances, persons arrested in the United States who have been suspected of terrorist activity on behalf of Al Qaeda or affiliated groups have not been placed in military detention pursuant to the AUMF, but instead have been prosecuted in federal court for criminal activity. There were two instances in which the Bush Administration transferred persons arrested in the United States into military custody and designated them as "enemy combatants"—one a U.S. citizen initially arrested by law enforcement authorities upon his return from Afghanistan, where he had allegedly been part of Taliban forces, and the other an alien present in the United States on a student visa who had never been to the Afghanistan zone of combat, but was alleged to have been an Al Qaeda "sleeper agent" planning to engage in terrorist activities on behalf of the organization within the United States. However, in both cases, the detainees were ultimately transferred back to the custody of civil authorities and tried in federal court when it appeared that the Supreme Court would hear their habeas petitions, leaving the legal validity of their prior military detention uncertain.[16]

Over the years, there has been considerable controversy over the appropriate mechanism for dealing with suspected belligerents and terrorists who come into U.S. custody. Some have argued that all suspected terrorists (or at least those believed to be affiliated with Al Qaeda) should be held in military custody and tried for any crimes they have committed before a military commission. Others have argued that such persons should be transferred to civilian law enforcement authorities and tried for any criminal offenses before an Article III court. Still others argue that neither a military nor traditional law enforcement model should serve as the exclusive

---

[12] Pamela Constable, *Karzai Orders "Full Afghanization" of U.S.-run Bagram Prison*, WASH. POST, November 29, 2012, at http://www.washingtonpost.com/world/karzai-orders-full-afghanization-of-us-run-bagram-prison/2012/11/19/39da5080-326e-11e2-92f0-496af208bf23_story.html.

[13] Karen DeYoung, *Parwan prison to be turned to Afghans, removing obstacle to long-term security agreement*, WASH. POST, March 23, 2013, at http://articles.washingtonpost.com/2013-03-23/world/37958352_1_parwan-prison-afghan-officials-afghan-civilians.

[14] Kevin Sieff, *In Afghanistan, a second Guantanamo*, WASH. POST, August 4, 2013, at http://www.washingtonpost.com/world/in-afghanistan-a-second-guantanamo/2013/08/04/e33e8658-f53e-11e2-81fa-8e83b3864c36_story.html?hpid=z1; Missy Ryan, *U.S. quietly moves detainees out of secretive Afghanistan prison*, REUTERS, June 12, 2014, at http://www.reuters.com/article/2014/06/12/us-usa-afghanistan-detainees-idUSKBN0EN2D820140612 (reporting that about 38 non-Afghan prisoners remain in the Parwan detention facility).

[15] U.S. Congress, Senate Committee on Armed Services, *Hearing to Consider the Nomination of Vice Admiral William H. McRaven, USN*, 112th Cong., 2nd sess., June 28, 2011, p. 43 [hereinafter "McRaven Testimony"], *transcript available at* http://armed-services.senate.gov/Transcripts/2011/06%20June/11-59%20-%206-28-11.pdf. Admiral McRaven indicated that captures outside a theater of operations like Iraq or Afghanistan are treated on a case-by-case basis.

[16] al-Marri v. Pucciarelli, 534 F.3d 213 (4th Cir. 2008) (per curiam), *cert. granted by* 555 U.S. 1066 (2008), *vacated and remanded for dismissal on mootness grounds by* al-Marri v. Spagone, 555 U.S. 1220 (2009); Padilla v. Hanft, 423 F.3d 386 (4th Cir. 2005). *See also* CRS Report R41156, *Judicial Activity Concerning Enemy Combatant Detainees: Major Court Rulings*, by Jennifer K. Elsea and Michael John Garcia (discussing *al-Marri* and *Padilla* litigation); CRS Report R42337, *Detention of U.S. Persons as Enemy Belligerents*, by Jennifer K. Elsea.

method for handling suspected terrorists and belligerents who come into U.S. custody. They urge that such decisions are best left to executive discretion for a decision based on the distinct facts of each case.

Disagreement over the appropriate model to employ has become a regular occurrence in high-profile cases involving suspected terrorists. In part as a response to the Obama Administration's plans to transfer certain Guantanamo detainees, including Khalid Sheik Mohammed, into the United States to face charges in an Article III court for their alleged role in the 9/11 attacks, Congress passed funding restrictions that effectively barred the transfer of any Guantanamo detainee into the United States for the 2011 fiscal year, even for purposes of criminal prosecution.[17] These restrictions have been extended through appropriations and defense authorization legislation enacted in subsequent years,[18] including pursuant to the 2014 NDAA and the Consolidated Appropriations Act, 2014 (2014 Omnibus; P.L. 113-76).[19] The blanket restriction on transfers into the United States effectively makes trial by military commission the only viable option for prosecuting Guantanamo detainees for the foreseeable future, as no civilian court operates at Guantanamo.

Considerable attention has also been drawn to other instances when terrorist suspects have been apprehended by U.S. military or civilian law enforcement authorities. On July 5, 2011, Somali national Ahmed Abdulkadir Warsame was brought to the United States to face terrorism-related charges in a civilian court, after having reportedly been detained on a U.S. naval vessel for two months for interrogation by military and intelligence personnel.[20] Some have argued that Warsame should have remained in military custody abroad, while others argue that he should have been transferred to civilian custody immediately. Controversy also arose regarding the arrest by U.S. civil authorities of Umar Farouk Abdulmutallab and Faisal Shahzad,[21] who some argued

---

[17] Ike Skelton National Defense Authorization Act for FY2011 (2011 NDAA), P.L. 111-383, §1032 (applying to military funds); Department of Defense and Full-Year Continuing Appropriations Act, 2011 (2011 CAA), P.L. 112-10, §1112 (applying to any funds appropriated by the 2011 CAA or any prior act). For further background, see CRS Report R40754, *Guantanamo Detention Center: Legislative Activity in the 111th Congress*, by Michael John Garcia.

[18] The Consolidated and Further Continuing Appropriations Act, 2012 (2012 Minibus; P.L. 112-55), and the Consolidated Appropriations Act, 2012 (2012 CAA; P.L. 112-74), extended this prohibition through the entirety of FY2012. *See* 2012 Minibus, P.L. 112-55, §532 (providing that "[n]one of the funds appropriated or otherwise made available in this or any other Act may be used to transfer, release, or assist in the transfer or release to or within the United States, its territories, or possessions" any detainee held at Guantanamo); 2012 CAA, P.L. 112-74, Div. A, §8119, Div. H, §511 (similar). In appropriations legislation, the phrase "or any other act" is typically interpreted as applying to any appropriation for the same fiscal year as the act in question. GOVERNMENT ACCOUNTABILITY OFFICE, OFFICE OF GENERAL COUNSEL, I PRINCIPLES OF APPROPRIATIONS LAW 2-36 (3d ed. 2004) (citing Williams v. United States, 240 F.3d 1019, 1063 (Fed. Cir. 2001) (Plager, J., dissenting)). The restrictions were effectively extended again until March 27, 2013, by the Continuing Appropriations Resolution, 2013 (2013 CAR; P.L. 112-175), and then for the duration of the fiscal year by the FY2013 Consolidated and Full Year Continuing Appropriations Act (P.L. 113-6) and the 2013 NDAA. *See* P.L. 113-6, Div. B, §530 and Div. C., §8109; 2013 NDAA, P.L. 112-239, §1027.

[19] National Defense Authorization Act for Fiscal Year 2014 (2014 NDAA), P.L. 113-66, §1034; Consolidated Appropriations Act, 2014 (2014 Omnibus), P.L. 113-76, Div. B., §528, Div. C, §8110, and Div. G, §537.

[20] Peter Finn and Karen DeYoung, *In Detention Case, a Blend of Two Systems*, WASH. POST, July 6, 2011, at A02, *available at* http://www.washingtonpost.com/national/national-security/in-somali-terror-suspects-case-administration-blends-military-civilian-systems/2011/07/06/gIQAQ4AJ1H_story.html. Warsame subsequently pleaded guilty to each of the nine terrorism-related charges for which he was indicted. *See* Dept. of Justice, Press Release, "Manhattan U.S. Attorney Announces Guilty Plea Of Ahmed Warsame," March 23, 2013, *available at* http://www.justice.gov/usao/nys/pressreleases/March13/WarsameUnsealingPR.php?print=1 (announcing the unsealing of guilty plea made in December 2011).

[21] Umar Farouk Abdulmutallab is a Nigerian national accused of trying to destroy an airliner traveling from Amsterdam to Detroit on Christmas Day 2009. He was apprehended and interrogated by civilian law enforcement before being (continued...)

should have been detained and interrogated by military authorities and tried by military commission. The Administration incurred additional criticism for bringing civilian charges against two Iraqi refugees arrested in the United States on suspicion of having participated in insurgent activities in Iraq against U.S. military forces,[22] although the war in Iraq has generally been treated as separate from hostilities authorized by the AUMF, at least insofar as detainee operations are concerned. The decision of U.S. authorities to bring criminal charges against former Al Qaeda spokesman Sulaiman Abu Ghayth in civilian court following his arrest, rather than transferring him to military custody at Guantanamo, was criticized by some lawmakers.[23] Most recently, the capture of alleged Benghazi ringleader Ahmed Abu Khattalah has evoked calls for holding him for interrogation at the Guantanamo Bay detention facility and for possibly prosecuting him by military commission.[24]

The following sections address the current status of U.S. policies and legal authorities with respect to detainee matters that are addressed in the 2012 NDAA and subsequent defense authorization legislation. The first section addresses the scope of detention authority under the AUMF as the Administration views it and as it has developed in court cases. The following section provides an overview of current practice regarding initial status determinations and periodic reviews of detainee cases. The background ends with a discussion of recidivism concerns underlying current restrictions on transferring detainees from Guantanamo.

Scope of Detention Authority Conferred by the AUMF

Prior to passage of the 2012 NDAA, the AUMF constituted the primary legal basis supporting the detention of persons captured in the conflict with Al Qaeda and affiliated entities, but the scope of the detention authority it confers is not made plain by its terms, and accordingly can be subject to differing interpretations. Section 1021 of the 2012 NDAA appears intended to codify existing law, as interpreted and applied by the executive branch and the D.C. Circuit, and expressly disavows any construction that would limit or expand the President's detention authority under the AUMF. Accordingly, an understanding of the state of the law prior to passage may inform the interpretation of the NDAA provisions relating to detention authority.

The Obama Administration framed its detention authority under the AUMF in a March 13, 2009, court brief as follows:

> The President has the authority to detain persons that the President determines planned, authorized, committed, or aided the terrorist attacks that occurred on September 11, 2001, and persons who harbored those responsible for those attacks. The President also has the authority to detain persons who were part of, or substantially supported, Taliban or al-Qaida forces or associated forces that are engaged in hostilities against the United States or its

---

(...continued)

charged in an Article III court, where he was sentenced to life imprisonment. Faisal Shahzad, a naturalized U.S. citizen originally from Pakistan, was arrested by civilian law enforcement and convicted in federal court for his attempt to detonate a bomb in New York's Times Square in 2010.

[22] *See* Jeremy Pelofsky, *US Lawmaker Wants Accused Iraqis Sent to Guantanamo*, REUTERS NEWS, June 14, 2011.

[23] *See* Michael Martinez, *Is Civilian or Military Justice Best for Osama bin Laden's Son-in-Law?*, CNN ONLINE, March 8, 2013 (quoting views of Senators McConnell, Graham, and Ayotte).

[24] *See* CRS Legal Sidebar WSLG969, Can Ahmed Abu Khattalah be Held at Guantanamo or Tried by Military Commission?, by Jennifer K. Elsea.

coalition partners, including any person who has committed a belligerent act, or has directly supported hostilities, in aid of such enemy armed forces.[25]

While membership in Al Qaeda or the Taliban seems to fall clearly within the parameters of the AUMF, the inclusion of "associated forces," a category of indeterminate breadth, raised questions as to whether the detention authority claimed by the executive exceeded the AUMF's mandate. The "substantial support" prong of the executive's description of its detention authority may raise similar questions. The Supreme Court in *Hamdi* interpreted the detention authority conferred by the AUMF with reference to law of war principles, and there is some dispute as to when and whether persons may be subject to indefinite detention under the law of war solely on account of providing support to a belligerent force.[26] In its 2009 brief, the government declined to clarify these aspects of its detention authority: "It is neither possible nor advisable, however, to attempt to identify, in the abstract, the precise nature and degree of 'substantial support,' or the precise characteristics of 'associated forces,' that are or would be sufficient to bring persons and organizations within the foregoing framework."[27]

The Obama Administration's definition of its scope of detention authority is similar to the Bush Administration's definition describing who could be treated as an "enemy combatant," differing only in that it requires "substantial support," rather than "support."[28] The controlling plurality opinion in *Hamdi* quoted with apparent approval a government brief in that case describing the authority to detain persons who support enemy forces, but suggested that such support would also entail engaging in hostilities.[29] Court decisions have not shed much light on the "substantial support" prong of the test to determine detention eligibility, with all cases thus far adjudicated by the Court of Appeals of the D.C. Circuit relying on proof that a detainee was functionally part of Al Qaeda, the Taliban, or an associated force.[30]

---

[25] *See In re* Guantanamo Bay Detainee Litigation, Respondents' Memorandum Regarding the Government's Detention Authority Relative to Detainees Held at Guantanamo Bay, No. 08-0442, filed March 13, 2009 (D.D.C.)(hereinafter "Government Brief"). This government brief is posted on the Department of Justice website at http://www.justice.gov/opa/documents/memo-re-det-auth.pdf.

[26]*Compare* Hamlily v. Obama, 616 F. Supp. 2d 63 (D.D.C. 2009) (finding that detention on account of providing substantial or direct support to a belligerent, without more, is inconsistent with the laws of war), *abrogated by* Al-Bihani v. Obama, 590 F.3d 866 (D.C. Cir. 2010) *with* Ryan Goodman, *The Detention of Civilians in Armed Conflict*, 103 A.J.I.L. 48 (2009) (discussing instances where the laws of war permit the detention of persons who have not directly participated in hostilities, including persons posing a security threat on account of their "indirect participation in hostilities," albeit as civilians rather than combatants). *See also* Allison M. Danner, *Defining Unlawful Enemy Combatants: A Centripetal Story*, 43 TEX. INT'L L.J. 1 (2007) (suggesting that the justification for detaining persons for providing "support" to Al Qaeda or the Taliban is influenced by principles of U.S. criminal law).

[27] Government Brief, *supra* footnote 25, at 2. The government also claimed that the contours of the definition of "associated forces" would require further development through their "application to concrete facts in individual cases." *Id.*

[28] *See* Parhat v. Gates, 532 F.3d 834, 838 (D.C. Cir. 2008) (quoting definition used in the order establishing Combatant Status Review Tribunals: "an individual who was part of or supporting Taliban or al Qaida forces, or associated forces that are engaged in hostilities against the United States or its coalition partners. This includes any person who has committed a belligerent act or has directly supported hostilities in aid of enemy armed forces.")

[29] Hamdi v. Rumsfeld, 542 U.S. 507, 519 (2004) (O'Connor, J., plurality opinion) ("A citizen, no less than an alien, can be 'part of or supporting forces hostile to the United States or coalition partners' *and* 'engaged in an armed conflict against the United States'; such a citizen, if released, would pose the same threat of returning to the front during the ongoing conflict.") (emphasis added; citation omitted).

[30] *See* CRS Report R41156, *Judicial Activity Concerning Enemy Combatant Detainees: Major Court Rulings*, by Jennifer K. Elsea and Michael John Garcia.

The executive branch has included "associated forces" as part of its description of the scope of its detention authority since at least 2004, after a majority of the Supreme Court held in *Hamdi* that the AUMF authorized the detention of enemy combatants for the duration of hostilities.[31] The Court left to lower courts the task of defining the full parameters of the detention authority conferred by the AUMF, and it did not mention "associated forces" in its opinion.[32] In its 2009 brief, the government explained that

> [The AUMF does not] limit the "organizations" it covers to just al-Qaida or the Taliban. In Afghanistan, many different private armed groups trained and fought alongside al-Qaida and the Taliban. In order "to prevent any future acts of international terrorism against the United States," AUMF, § 2(a), the United States has authority to detain individuals who, in analogous circumstances in a traditional international armed conflict between the armed forces of opposing governments, would be detainable under principles of co-belligerency.[33]

This statement is consistent with the position earlier taken by the Bush Administration with respect to the detention of a group of Chinese Uighur dissidents who had been captured in Afghanistan and transferred to Guantanamo as members of an "associated force." In *Parhat v. Gates*,[34] the D.C. Circuit rejected the government's contention that one petitioner's alleged affiliation with the East Turkistan Islamic Movement (ETIM) made him an "enemy combatant." The court accepted the government's test for membership in an "associated force" (which was not disputed by petitioner): "(1) the petitioner was part of or supporting 'forces'; (2) those forces were associated with al Qaida or the Taliban; and (3) those forces are engaged in hostilities against the United States or its coalition partners."[35]

The court did not find that the government's evidence supported the second and third prongs, so it found it unnecessary to reach the first. The government had defined "associated force" to be one that "becomes so closely associated with al Qaida or the Taliban that it is effectively 'part of the same organization,'" in which case it argued ETIM is covered by the AUMF because that force

---

[31] Hamdi v. Rumsfeld, 542 U.S. 507 (2004). A plurality of the Supreme Court stated,

> The AUMF authorizes the President to use "all necessary and appropriate force" against "nations, organizations, or persons" associated with the September 11, 2001, terrorist attacks. 115 Stat. 224. There can be no doubt that individuals who fought against the United States in Afghanistan as part of the Taliban, an organization known to have supported the al Qaeda terrorist network responsible for those attacks, are individuals Congress sought to target in passing the AUMF. We conclude that detention of individuals falling into the limited category we are considering, for the duration of the particular conflict in which they were captured, is so fundamental and accepted an incident to war as to be an exercise of the "necessary and appropriate force" Congress has authorized the President to use.

Id. at 518 (O'Connor, J., plurality opinion). *See also id.* at 587 (Thomas, J., dissenting) (agreeing with plurality that AUMF authorizes the President to detain enemy forces).

[32] The plurality cited with apparent approval the declaration of a government official in explaining why the petitioner, who had surrendered to the Northern Alliance in Afghanistan, was considered to be an "enemy combatant":

> [B]ecause al Qaeda and the Taliban "were and are hostile forces engaged in armed conflict with the armed forces of the United States," "individuals associated with" those groups "were and continue to be enemy combatants."

Id. at 514 (O'Connor, J., plurality opinion).

[33] *See* Government Brief, *supra* footnote 25, at 7. One D.C. district judge expressly adopted the "co-belligerency" test for defining which organizations may be deemed "associated forces" under the AUMF, *see* Hamlily v. Obama, 616 F. Supp. 2d 63, 74-75 (D.D.C. 2009), but it does not appear that the D.C. Circuit has adopted that view.

[34] 532 F.3d 834 (D.C. Cir. 2008) (court challenge under now defunct Detainee Treatment Act judicial review process).

[35] *Id.* at 843 (citations omitted).

"thereby becomes the same 'organization[ ]' that perpetrated the September 11 attacks." If the definition asserted by the government in *Parhat* is adopted, then the term would seem to require a close operational nexus in the current armed conflict. On the other hand, as the court noted, "[t]his argument suggests that, even under the government's own definition, the evidence must establish a connection between ETIM and al Qaida or the Taliban that is considerably closer than the relationship suggested by the usual meaning of the word 'associated.'"[36] The court did not find that the evidence adduced established that ETIM is sufficiently connected to Al Qaeda to be an "associated force," as the government had defined the concept, but the decision might have come out differently if the court had adopted a plain language interpretation of "associated force."

In its 2009 brief, the government indicated that the definition of "associated forces" would require further development through its "application to concrete facts in individual cases."[37] In habeas cases so far, the term "associated forces" appears to have been interpreted only to cover armed groups assisting the Taliban or Al Qaeda in Afghanistan. For instance, membership in "Zubayda's militia," which reportedly assisted Osama bin Laden's escape from Tora Bora, has been found to be an "associated force" within the meaning of the AUMF.[38] In another case, the habeas court determined that Hezb-i–Islami Gulbuddin (HIG) is an "associated force" for AUMF purposes because there was sufficient evidence to show that it supported continued attacks against coalition and Afghan forces at the time petitioner was captured.[39] The D.C. Circuit also affirmed the detention of a person engaged as a cook for the 55th Arab Military Brigade, an armed force consisting of mostly foreign fighters that defended the Taliban from coalition efforts to oust it from power.[40] However, the Administration has suggested that other groups outside of Afghanistan may be considered "associated forces" such that the AUMF authorizes the use of force against their members.[41] It is possible that Congress's codification of the detention authority as to "associated forces" in the 2012 NDAA may bring courts to interpret the term more broadly than they have in the past in order to comport with the plain text meaning.

An issue of continuing uncertainty regarding the scope of detention authority conferred by the AUMF concerns its application to persons captured outside of Afghanistan, and in particular those who are U.S. citizens or otherwise have significant ties to the United States. While the Supreme Court in *Hamdi* recognized that the AUMF permitted the detention of a U.S. citizen captured while fighting U.S. coalition forces in Afghanistan, it did not address whether (or the circumstances in which) persons captured outside of Afghanistan could be properly detained under the AUMF. The U.S. Court of Appeals for the D.C. Circuit has apparently taken the view

---

[36] *Id.* at 844. The court noted the following exchange that had taken place at an oral hearing:

> Judge Sentelle: So you are dependent on the proposition that ETIM is properly defined as being part of al Qaida, not that it aided or abetted, or aided or harbored al Qaida, but that it's part of [?]
>
> Mr. Katsas: Correct ... in order to fit them in the AUMF.

Id. and footnote 4.

[37] *Id.*

[38] *See* Barhoumi v. Obama, 609 F.3d 416 (D.C. Cir. 2010).

[39] Khan v. Obama, 646 F. Supp. 2d 6 (D.D.C. 2009). *See also* Khan v. Obama, 655 F.3d 20 (D.C. Cir. 2011) (in review of lower court ruling in same litigation, affirming district court's determination that HIG is an "associated force" within the meaning of the AUMF).

[40] Al-Bihani v. Obama, 590 F.3d 866, *en banc rehearing denied*, 619 F.3d 1 (D.C. Cir. 2010), *cert. denied*, 131 S. Ct. 1814 (2011).

[41] *See* Harold Hongju Koh, Legal Adviser, U.S. Department of State, The Obama Administration and International Law, Address at the Annual Meeting of the American Society of International Law, Washington, D.C. (March 25, 2010), *available at* http://www.state.gov/s/l/releases/remarks/139119.htm.

that the AUMF authorizes the detention of any person who is functionally part of Al Qaeda, though this view has been espoused so far only in cases involving non-U.S. citizens who have been captured outside the United States.[42] In separate rulings, the U.S. Court of Appeals for the Fourth Circuit upheld the military detention of a U.S. citizen and a lawfully admitted alien captured in the United States who were designated as enemy combatants by the executive branch.[43] In each case, the detainee was transferred to civilian law enforcement custody for criminal prosecution before the Supreme Court could consider the merits of the case. In one of these cases, the lower court's decision upholding the detention was vacated.[44] The other case affirming such a detention remains good law within the Fourth Circuit, but relied on conduct outside the United States as the basis for detention.[45] Accordingly, the circumstances in which a U.S. citizen or other person captured or arrested in the United States may be detained under the authority conferred by the AUMF remains unsettled.[46] The 2012 NDAA does not disturb the state of the law in this regard.

Status Determinations for Unprivileged Enemy Belligerents

In response to Supreme Court decisions in 2004 related to "enemy combatants," the Pentagon established Combatant Status Review Tribunals (CSRTs) to determine whether detainees brought to Guantanamo are subject to detention on account of enemy belligerency status. CSRTs are an administrative and non-adversarial process based on the procedures the Army uses to determine POW status during traditional wars.[47] Guantanamo detainees who were determined not to be (or no longer to be) enemy combatants were eligible for transfer to their country of citizenship or were otherwise dealt with "consistent with domestic and international obligations and U.S. foreign policy."[48] CSRTs confirmed the status of 539 enemy combatants between July 30, 2004,

---

[42] *See, e.g.*, Bensayah v. Obama, 610 F.3d 718 (D.C. Cir. 2010) (recognizing that government might be able to lawfully detain an Algerian citizen arrested by Bosnian authorities in 2001 and subsequently transferred to U.S. custody for detention at Guantanamo, but remanding to lower court to assess sufficiency of government's evidence that petitioner was a member of Al Qaeda); Salahi v. Obama, 625 F.3d 745 (D.C. Cir. 2010) (in assessing whether person captured in Mauritania was lawfully detained under the AUMF, "the relevant inquiry is whether [the petitioner] was 'part of' al-Qaida when captured").

[43] Padilla v. Hanft, 423 F.3d 386 (4th Cir. 2005); al-Marri v. Pucciarelli, 534 F.3d 213 (4th Cir. 2008).

[44] al-Marri v. Pucciarelli, 534 F.3d 213 (4th Cir. 2008), *vacated* and remanded for dismissal on mootness grounds by al-Marri v. Spagone, 555 U.S. 1220 (2009).

[45] Padilla v. Hanft, 423 F.3d 386, 390-391 (4th Cir. 2005)(holding that U.S. citizen captured in the United States could be detained pursuant to the AUMF because he had been, prior to returning to the country, "'armed and present in a combat zone' in Afghanistan as part of Taliban forces during the conflict there with the United States").

[46] For analysis of historical practice relating to the wartime detention of U.S. citizens, see CRS Report R42337, *Detention of U.S. Persons as Enemy Belligerents*, by Jennifer K. Elsea.

[47] *See* Department of Defense Fact Sheet, "Combatant Status Review Tribunals," *available at* http://www.defenselink.mil/news/Jul2004/d20040707factsheet.pdf. CSRT proceedings are modeled on the procedures of Army Regulation (AR) 190-8, Enemy Prisoners of War, Retained Personnel, Civilian Internees and Other Detainees (1997), which establishes administrative procedures to determine the status of detainees under the Geneva Conventions and prescribes their treatment in accordance with international law. It does not include a category for "unlawful" or "enemy" combatants, who would presumably be covered by the other categories.

[48] *See* Department of Defense Press Release, "Combatant Status Review Tribunal Order Issued" (June 7, 2004), *available at* http://www.defense.gov/releases/release.aspx?releaseid=7530; Memorandum from the Deputy Secretary of Defense to the Secretary of the Navy, Order Establishing Combatant Status Review Tribunal, July 7, 2004 (hereinafter "CSRT Order"), *available at* http://www.defenselink mil/news/Jul2004/d20040707review.pdf; Memorandum from Deputy Secretary of Defense, Implementation of Combatant Status Review Tribunals Procedures for Enemy Combatants Detained at U.S. Naval Base Guantanamo Bay, Cuba, July 14, 2006 (hereinafter "CSRT Implementing Directive"), *available at* http://www.defenselink mil/news/Aug2006/d20060809CSRTProcedures.pdf.

---

and February 10, 2009.[49] Although the CSRT process has been largely defunct since 2007 due to the fact that so few detainees have been brought to Guantanamo since that time,[50] presumably any new detainees who might be transported to the Guantanamo detention facility would go before a CSRT. The CSRT process has only been employed with respect to persons held at Guantanamo. Non-citizen detainees held by the United States in Afghanistan have been subject to a different status review process which provides detainees with fewer procedural rights.[51] Moreover, whereas the Supreme Court has held that the constitutional writ of habeas extends to non-citizens held at Guantanamo,[52] enabling Guantanamo detainees to challenge the legality of their detention in federal court, existing lower court jurisprudence has not recognized that a similar privilege extends to non-citizen detainees held by the United States in Afghanistan.[53]

Shortly after taking office, President Obama issued a series of executive orders creating a number of task forces to study issues related to the Guantanamo detention facility and U.S. detention policy generally. While these groups prepared their studies, most proceedings related to military commission and administrative review boards at Guantanamo, including the CSRTs, were held in abeyance pending the anticipated recommendations. The Obama Administration also announced in 2009 that it was implementing a new review system to determine or review the status of detainees held at the Bagram Theater Internment Facility in Afghanistan,[54] which also applied at the detention facility in Parwan.[55] It is unclear what process has been used to determine the status of persons captured in connection with the hostilities who were not transported to any of those facilities.[56]

---

[49] *See* Department of Defense, Combatant Status Review Tribunal Summary, February 10, 2009 [hereinafter "CSRT Summary"], *available at* http://www.defense.gov/news/csrtsummary.pdf. Nearly all CSRT proceedings were held in 2004, another two dozen were held in 2005, none took place in 2006, fourteen were held in 2007 (likely the fourteen "high-value" detainees, including Khalid Sheik Mohammed and others previously detained by the CIA), with numbers dropping off significantly after that time. For more information about the CSRT rules and procedures, see CRS Report RL33180, *Enemy Combatant Detainees: Habeas Corpus Challenges in Federal Court*, by Jennifer K. Elsea and Michael John Garcia.

[50] *See* Guantanamo Review Task Force, Final Report 1, January 22, 2010, *available at* http://www.justice.gov/ag/guantanamo-review-final-report.pdf (reporting statistics related to arrivals at Guantanamo). CSRTs continue to be held in the event that "new evidence" is received that may affect a detainee's initial status determination, but these were temporarily suspended in 2009 along with the suspension of the Annual Administrative Review process. *See* CSRT Summary, *supra* footnote 49.

[51] *See generally*, Maqaleh v. Gates, 604 F. Supp. 2d 205, 226-228 (D.D.C. 2009)(comparing CSRT process with that employed at Bagram detention facility prior to 2009), *vacated on other grounds and remanded by* 605 F.3d 84 (D.C. Cir. 2010); Jeff A. Bovarnick, *Detainee Review Boards in Afghanistan: From Strategic Liability to Legitimacy*, ARMY LAW., June 2010, at 9 (discussing evolution of the detainee review process used by the United States in Afghanistan); Letter from Phillip Carter, Dep. Asst. Sec. Defense for Detainee Policy, to Sen. Carl Levin, Chairman of Sen. Armed Serv. Comm., July 14, 2009, *available at* http://www.scotusblog.com/wp/wp-content/uploads/2009/09/US-Bagram-brief-9-14-09.pdf (discussing 2009 modifications to the status review process employed with respect to persons held by the United States at Bagram).

[52] Boumediene v. Bush, 553 U.S. 723 (2008).

[53] *See* Maqaleh v. Gates, 605 F.3d 84 (D.C. Cir. 2010) (holding that, at least as a general matter, the constitutional writ of habeas does not extend to non-citizens detained in the Afghan theater of war).

[54] Karen DeYoung and Peter Finn, *New Review System Will Give Afghan Prisoners More Rights*, WASH. POST, September 13, 2009. The new system reportedly gave the detainees certain rights that were unavailable to detainees subject to the "Unlawful Enemy Combatant Review Board" established in 2007, including a limited right to call witnesses and examine government information, and a right to have the assistance of a personal military representative.

[55] *See* Daniel, *supra* footnote 10.

[56] Admiral McRaven, discussing this issue at his confirmation hearing for command of SOCOM, noted that Guantanamo is "off the table" as a prospective destination for persons newly captured in hostilities against Al Qaeda, (continued...)

On March 7, 2011, President Obama issued Executive Order 13567, establishing a process for the periodic review of the continued detention of persons currently held at Guantanamo who have either been (1) designated for preventive detention under the laws of war or (2) referred for criminal prosecution, but have not been convicted of a crime and do not have formal charges pending against them.[57] The executive order establishes a Periodic Review Board (PRB) to assess whether the continued detention of a covered individual is warranted in order "to protect against a significant threat to the security of the United States." In instances where a person's continued detention is not deemed warranted, the Secretaries of State and Defense are designated responsibility "for ensuring that vigorous efforts are undertaken to identify a suitable transfer location for any such detainee, outside of the United States, consistent with the national security and foreign policy interests of the United States" and relevant legal requirements. An initial review of each individual covered by the order, which involves a hearing before the PRB in which the detainee and his representative may challenge the government's basis for his continued detention and introduce evidence on his own behalf, was required to occur within a year of the order's issuance. The order requires a full review thereafter on a triennial basis and a file review every six months in intervening years, which could, if significant new information is revealed therein, result in a new full review. The order also specifies that the process it establishes is discretionary; does not create any additional basis for detention authority or modify the scope of authority granted under existing law; and is not intended to affect federal courts' jurisdiction to determine the legality of a person's continued detention. The one-year deadline established by the executive order for the initial review of covered persons' continued detention was not met. In May 2012, the Department of Defense issued a directive that establishes guidelines for the implementation of the periodic review process, but it was not until July 2013 that it was announced that the first periodic review boards would take place.[58] An announcement of the completion of the first PRB process occurred on January 9, 2014.[59]

"Recidivism" and Restrictions on Transfer

Concerns that detainees released from Guantanamo to their home country or resettled elsewhere have subsequently engaged in terrorist activity have spurred Congress to place limits on detainee transfers, generally requiring a certification that adequate measures are put in place in the destination country to prevent transferees from "returning to the battlefield."[60] Statistics regarding the post-release activities of Guantanamo detainees have been somewhat elusive, however, with much of the information remaining classified. It does not appear to be disputed that some

(...continued)

and that sovereignty issues make it unlikely that persons captured outside Afghanistan will be transferred to Parwan for detention. *See* McRaven Testimony, *supra* footnote 15. Admiral McRaven indicated that captures outside a theater of operations like Iraq or Afghanistan are treated on a case-by-case basis, with detainees sometimes kept on board a naval vessel until a decision is made, *id.* at 37, but did not indicate what if any process is used to determine the detainee's status as subject to detention under the AUMF in the first place.

[57] Exec. Order No. 13,567, "Periodic Review of Individuals Detained at Guantanamo Bay Naval Station Pursuant to Authorization to Use Military Force," 76 Fed. Reg. 13,277 (March 10, 2011) [hereinafter "Executive Order on Periodic Review"].

[58] Carol Rosenberg, *71 Guantanamo prisoners will get parole-style hearings, Pentagon says*, WASH. POST, July 22, 2013, at A4.

[59] Department of Defense Press Release, "Completion of First Guantanamo Periodic Review Board," January 9, 2014, *available at* http://www.defense.gov/releases/release.aspx?releaseid=16473.

[60] For an overview of restrictions, see CRS Report R40754, *Guantanamo Detention Center: Legislative Activity in the 111th Congress*, by Michael John Garcia.

detainees have engaged in terrorist activities of some kind after their release from Guantanamo, but the significance of such activity has been subject to debate. The policy implications of the reported activities have also been the subject of controversy, with some arguing that virtually none of the remaining prisoners should be transferred and others arguing that long-term detention without trial of such persons, based on the conduct of others who have been released, is fundamentally unfair.

In 2007, the Pentagon issued a news release estimating that 30 former detainees had since their release engaged in militant activities or "anti-U.S. propaganda" (apparently including public criticism of U.S. detention policies).[61] This number and others released by DOD officials were challenged by researchers at Seton Hall University School of Law Center for Policy and Research who, in connection with advocacy on behalf of some Guantanamo detainees pursuing habeas cases, identified what they viewed as discrepancies in DOD data as well as a lack of identifying information that would enable independent verification of the numbers.[62] Moreover, they took issue with the Pentagon's assertion that the former detainees' activities could be classified as "recidivism" or "reengagement," inasmuch as data released by the Pentagon from CSRT hearings did not establish in each case that the detainee had engaged in terrorist or insurgent activity in the first place, and suggested that post-release terrorist conduct could potentially be explained by radicalization during internment. The study did note that available data confirmed some cases of individuals who engaged in deadly activities such as suicide bombings after leaving Guantanamo.

In 2008, the Defense Intelligence Agency (DIA) reported that 36 ex-Guantanamo detainees were confirmed or suspected of having returned to terrorism.[63] In 2009, the Pentagon reported that 1 in 7, or 74 of the 534 prisoners transferred from Guantanamo were believed to have subsequently engaged in terrorism or militant activity.[64]

More recent estimates by the executive branch, sometimes made publicly available through legislative action, have provided different numbers. In December 2010, pursuant to a requirement contained in the Intelligence Authorization Act of FY2010 (P.L. 111-259), the Director of National Intelligence (DNI) released an unclassified summary of intelligence relating to recidivism rates of current or former Guantanamo detainees, as well as an assessment of the likelihood that such detainees may engage in terrorism or communicate with terrorist

---

[61] Department of Defense, "Former Guantanamo Detainees Who Have Returned to the Fight," news release, July 12, 2007.

[62] *See* Mark Denbeaux et al., *The Meaning of "Battlefield"* (2007), *available at* http://law.shu.edu/publications/ guantanamoReports/meaning_of_battlefield_final_121007.pdf; *see also* Mark Denbeaux et al., *Released Guantánamo Detainees and the Department of Defense: Propaganda by the Numbers?* (2009), *available at* http://law.shu.edu/ publications/guantanamoReports/propaganda_numbers_11509.pdf.

[63] Department of Defense, Fact Sheet: Former GTMO Detainee Terrorism Trends (June 13, 2008), *available at* http://www.defense.gov/news/d20080613Returntothefightfactsheet.pdf. The factsheet described "confirmed" as being demonstrated by a "preponderance of evidence," such as "fingerprints, DNA, conclusive photographic match, or reliable, verified, or well-corroborated intelligence reporting." It described "suspected" as "[s]ignificant reporting indicates a former Defense Department detainee is involved in terrorist activities, and analysis indicates the detainee most likely is associated with a specific former detainee *or* unverified or single-source, but plausible, reporting indicates a specific former detainee is involved in terrorist activities." (Emphasis in original). The document does not indicate how many of the total number fell into each category.

[64] Elisabeth Bumiller, *Later Terror Link Cited for 1 in 7 Freed Detainees*, NY TIMES, May 20, 2009, *available at* http://www.nytimes.com/2009/05/21/us/politics/21gitmo.html. The report noted that 27 of the former prisoners were confirmed as having engaged in terrorism, while the remaining 47 were merely suspected of doing so. *Id.* (editor's note).

---

organizations. The report stated that of the 598 detainees transferred out of Guantanamo, the "Intelligence Community assesses that 81 (13.5 percent) are confirmed and 69 (11.5 percent) are suspected of reengaging in terrorist or insurgent activities after transfer."[65] Of the 150 confirmed or suspected recidivist detainees, the report stated that 13 are dead, 54 are in custody, and 83 remain at large. The summary also indicated that, of 66 detainees transferred from Guantanamo since the implementation of Executive Order 13492,[66] 2 are confirmed and 3 are suspected of participating in terrorist or insurgent activities.[67] The report does not include detainees solely on the basis of anti-U.S. statements or writings.[68]

In September 2011, Director of National Intelligence Lieutenant General James Clapper testified in a congressional hearing that the number of former Guantanamo detainees who were either suspected or confirmed to have engaged in terrorist or insurgent activities upon release had risen to 27%.[69] In January 2012, the President signed into law the Intelligence Authorization Act of FY2012 (P.L. 112-87), which required the DNI to release another unclassified summary of intelligence relating to recidivism rates of current or former Guantanamo detainees, and to provide periodic updates not less than every six months thereafter.[70] The first summary was released in March 2012, and claimed that of the 599 detainees transferred out of Guantanamo by the end of 2011, 95 detainees (15.9%) were "confirmed of reengaging" in terrorist or insurgent activities, and 72 detainees (12.0%) were "suspected of reengaging" in such activities.[71] Of the 67 detainees transferred since the implementation of Executive Order 13492, 3 were confirmed and 2 were suspected of participating in terrorist or insurgent activities.[72] As with the earlier DNI estimate, the report does not identify detainees as "reengaging" in terrorist or insurgent activity solely on the basis of anti-U.S. statements, or on account of communications with persons or organizations that are unrelated to terrorist operations.

The latest DNI recidivism summary, released in March 2014, states that out of a total of 614 detainees who have been transferred or released, 104 detainees have been confirmed of

---

[65] Office of the Director of National Intelligence, Summary of the Reengagement of Detainees Formerly Held at Guantanamo Bay, Cuba (December 2010) [hereinafter "2010 DNI Recidivism Summary"], *available at* http://www.dni.gov/electronic_reading_room/ 120710_Summary_of_the_Reengagement_of_Detainees_Formerly_Held_at_Guantanamo_Bay_Cuba.pdf.

[66] Exec. Order No. 13,492, Review and Disposition of Individuals Detained at the Guantanamo Bay Naval Base and Closure of Detention Facilities, 74 Fed. Reg. 4,897 (January 22, 2009).

[67] 2010 DNI Recidivism Summary, *supra* footnote 65.

[68] *Id.* The assessment defines "terrorist" or "insurgent" activities for its purposes as including "planning terrorist operations, conducting a terrorist or insurgent attack against Coalition or host-nation forces or civilians, conducting a suicide bombing, financing terrorist operations, recruiting others for terrorist operations, arranging for movement of individuals involved in terrorist operations, etc." but not communications on issues not related to terrorist operations or "writing anti-U.S. books or articles, or making anti-U.S. propaganda statements." *Id.*

[69] Lt. Gen. James Clapper, Director of National Intelligence, *The State of Intelligence Reform 10 Years After 9/11*, Joint Hearing of the Permanent Select Committee on Intelligence and the Senate Select Committee on Intelligence, U.S. House of Representatives, September 13, 2011. *See also* U.S. Congress, House Committee on Armed Services, Subcommittee on Oversight and Investigations, *Leaving Guantanamo: Policies, Pressures, and Detainees Returning to the Fight* (January 2012), *available at* http://armedservices.house.gov/index.cfm/files/serve?File_id=24338661-2a6d-49c6-b9a5-bb0721825a69/.

[70] Intelligence Authorization Act of FY2012, P.L. 112-87, §307.

[71] Office of the Director of National Intelligence, Summary of the Reengagement of Detainees Formerly Held at Guantanamo Bay, Cuba (March 2012), *available at* http://dni.gov/reports/ March%202012%20Summary%20of%20Reengagement.pdf.

[72] *Id.*

---

reengaging in terrorist or insurgent activity (raising the percentage of former detainees falling under this category to 16.9%), and 74 former detainees fall into the "suspected of reengaging" category (12.1% of former detainees).[73]

The accuracy or significance of the numbers provided by DNI and other government entities has been questioned by some observers. In response to the release of the 2010 DNI estimate, the New America Foundation analyzed publicly available Pentagon reports and other documents and estimated that the actual figure of released detainees who went on to pose a threat to the United States or its interests is closer to 6%.[74] Some have raised similar criticisms with respect to the accuracy of more recent DNI estimates.[75] Because the intelligence data forming the basis for the DNI's reports remain classified, it is not possible to explain the discrepancy between their estimates of detainee recidivism numbers and those estimates deriving from publicly available sources. At any rate, there seems to be broad agreement that the number of detainees who engage in activities related to terrorism after their release has grown.

2012 NDAA: Summary and Analysis of Detainee Provisions

Detention Authority

Section 1021 affirms that the AUMF includes authority for the U.S. Armed Forces to detain "covered persons" pending disposition under the law of war. The provision generally tracks the language of Senate-passed S. 1867, 112th Congress. Combining the express language of the AUMF with the language the Obama Administration has employed to describe its detention authority in habeas litigation involving Guantanamo detainees,[76] the 2012 NDAA defines "covered persons" in Section 1021(b) as including two categories of persons:

> (1) A person who planned, authorized, committed, or aided the terrorist attacks that occurred on September 11, 2001, or harbored those responsible for those attacks.
>
> (2) A person who was a part of or substantially supported al-Qaeda, the Taliban, or associated forces that are engaged in hostilities against the United States or its coalition partners, including any person who has committed a belligerent act or has directly supported such hostilities in aid of such enemy forces.[77]

---

[73] Office of the Director of National Intelligence, Summary of the Reengagement of Detainees Formerly Held at Guantanamo Bay, Cuba (as of January 14, 2014), *available at* http://www.dni.gov/files/documents/Newsroom/Reports%20and%20Pubs/GTMO.pdf.

[74] *See* Peter Bergen, Katherine Tiedemann, and Andrew Lebovich, *How Many Gitmo Alumni Take Up Arms?*, FOREIGN POLICY online, January 11, 2011, *available at* http://www foreignpolicy.com/articles/2011/01/11/how_many_gitmo_alumni_take_up_arms.

[75] *See* Andy Worthington, Future of Freedom Foundation, *Guantánamo and Recidivism: The Media's Ongoing Failure to Question Official Statistics*, March 13, 2012, *available at* http://www fff.org/comment/com1203k.asp.

[76] *See supra*, discussion in "Scope of Detention Authority Conferred by the AUMF."

[77] The earlier version of Section 1021 contained in S. 1253 (in that bill numbered Section 1031) had included similar language defining "covered persons," but rather than "affirming" detention authority under the AUMF, it directly authorized the Armed Forces to detain covered persons "captured in the course of hostilities authorized by the [AUMF] as unprivileged enemy belligerents," and permitted their detention until "the end of hostilities against the nations, (continued...)

Section 1021 states that dispositions under the law of war "may include" several options:

- detention without trial until the end of hostilities authorized by the 2001 AUMF;
- trial by military commission;
- transfer for trial by another court or tribunal with jurisdiction; or
- transfer to the custody or control of a foreign country or foreign entity.

The provision uses the language "may include" with respect to the above options, which could be read as permission to add other options or negate any of the listed options.[78]

Section 1021 does not expressly clarify whether U.S. citizens or lawful resident aliens may be determined to be "covered persons." The potential application of an earlier version of Section 1021 found in S. 1867 (in that bill numbered Section 1031) to U.S. citizens and other persons within the United States was the subject of significant floor debate. An amendment that would have expressly barred U.S. citizens from long-term military detention on account of enemy belligerent status was considered and rejected.[79] Ultimately, an amendment was adopted that added the following proviso: "Nothing in this section shall be construed to affect existing law or authority relating to the detention of United States citizens, lawful resident aliens of the United States, or any other persons who are captured or arrested in the United States."[80]

This language, which remains in the final version of the act,[81] along with a separate clause which provides that nothing in Section 1021 "is intended to limit or expand the authority of the

---

(...continued)

organizations, and persons subject to the [AUMF]." The White House reportedly objected to the language "captured in the course of hostilities" because it could be read to limit detentions to those captured during military operations and not persons who are arrested under other circumstances. *See* Charlie Savage, *Levin and McCain Strike Deal Over Detainee Handling*, THE CAUCUS (BLOG) NY TIMES (November 15, 2011, 3:19 PM), http://thecaucus.blogs.nytimes.com/2011/11/15/levin-and-mccain-strike-deal-over-detainee-handling/.

[78] During the Senate floor debate over S. 1867 (112th Cong.), an amendment offered by Senator Sessions to clarify that an acquittal by a federal court or military commission would not preclude continued detention under the law of war was not adopted. S.Amdt. 1274 (not agreed to by a vote of 41-59).

[79] S.Amdt. 1126 (seeking to bar the long-term military detention of U.S. citizens) (not agreed to by a vote of 45-55).

[80] S.Amdt. 1456.

[81] The language was amended slightly in conference by adding commas. With or without the commas, it is unclear whether U.S. citizens or lawful resident aliens are meant to be covered only if they are captured or arrested in the United States, or whether the place of arrest is important only with respect to "other persons." Accordingly, the provision might be interpreted as conferring broader detention authority with respect to U.S. citizens and lawful resident aliens who are captured *abroad* than what was originally included in the AUMF (though Section 1021(d) of the 2012 NDAA states that Section 1021 is not intended to limit or expand either the President's authority to detain persons or scope of the authority conferred by the AUMF). The Court of Appeals for the Second Circuit has interpreted the phrase to cover U.S. citizens and lawful resident aliens irrespective of location. Hedges v. Obama, 724 F.3d170 (2d Cir. 2013), *cert. denied*, 134 S. Ct. 1936 (2014). The Supreme Court's decision in *Hamdi* seems to establish clear detention authority with respect to those who engaged in relevant hostilities overseas, but not with respect to those captured in other circumstances. The D.C. Circuit, however, has not required proof that a detainee actually engaged in hostilities in order to affirm detention authority, and would likely apply the same definitional analysis to U.S. citizens and resident aliens that it has applied to aliens detained at Guantanamo. U.S. persons detained under the authority would be able to challenge their detention by petitioning for habeas corpus, even if they are detained abroad outside of Guantanamo. Whether the courts will accord U.S. citizens or resident aliens the same procedural rights that the D.C. Circuit has deemed appropriate for aliens detained at Guantanamo remains to be seen, if in fact any such persons are detained under the provision.

President or the scope of the Authorization for the Use of Military Force," makes clear that the provision is not intended to either expand or limit the executive's existing authority to detain U.S. citizens and resident aliens, as well as other persons captured in the United States. Such detentions have been rare and subject to substantial controversy, without achieving definitive resolution in the courts. While the Supreme Court in *Hamdi* recognized that persons captured while fighting U.S. forces in Afghanistan could be militarily detained in the conflict with Al Qaeda potentially for the duration of hostilities, regardless of their citizenship, the circumstances in which persons captured in the United States may be subject to preventive military detention have not been definitively adjudicated.[82] Section 1021 does not attempt to clarify the circumstances in which a U.S. citizen, lawful resident alien, or other person captured within the United States may be held as an enemy belligerent in the conflict with Al Qaeda. Consequently, if the executive branch decides to hold such a person under the detention authority affirmed in Section 1021, it is left to the courts to decide whether Congress meant to authorize such detention when it enacted the AUMF in 2001.[83]

In restating the definitional standard the Administration uses to characterize its detention authority, Section 1021 does not attempt to provide additional clarification for terms such as "substantial support," "associated forces," or "hostilities." For that reason, it may be subject to an evolving interpretation that effectively permits a broadening of the scope of the conflict. The provision does require the Secretary of Defense to brief Congress on how it is applied, including with respect to "organizations, entities, and individuals considered to be 'covered persons' under section 1021(b)." This language may be read to require an ongoing accounting of which entities are considered to be "associated forces" or a description of what constitutes "substantial support."

Although Section 1021 provides that it does not modify any existing detention authority concerning "lawful resident aliens," neither the NDAA nor any other federal statute provides a definition of this term.[84] It is possible that the drafters of the NDAA intended this category to refer to the classification of aliens known as legal permanent residents (LPRs). Aliens with LPR status are allowed to permanently reside in the United States, unless such status terminates as a result of a final order of removal or exclusion. On the other hand, it is possible that the drafters of

---

[82] In separate rulings, the U.S. Court of Appeals for the Fourth Circuit upheld the military detention of a U.S. citizen and a resident alien captured in the United States and designated as enemy combatants by the executive branch. Padilla v. Hanft, 423 F.3d 386, 390-391 (4th Cir. 2005)(holding that U.S. citizen captured in the United States could be detained pursuant to the AUMF because he had been, prior to returning to the country, "'armed and present in a combat zone' in Afghanistan as part of Taliban forces during the conflict there with the United States"); al-Marri v. Pucciarelli, 534 F.3d 213 (4th Cir. 2008), *vacated by* al-Marri v. Spagone, 129 S.Ct. 1545 (2009). In each case, the detainee was transferred to civilian law enforcement custody for criminal prosecution before the Supreme Court could consider the merits of the case. *See also* "Scope of Detention Authority Conferred by the AUMF."

[83] In the case of a resident alien detained on the basis of activity conducted within the United States that could bring the person within the purview of the mandatory detention provision in Section 1022, the President may have to first determine whether the detention is constitutional in order to establish whether military custody is in fact mandated pursuant to Section 1022.

[84] Although the Immigration and Nationality Act (INA) contains a definition of "residence" for immigration purposes and the Internal Revenue Code defines "resident alien" for tax purposes, these definitions are not coextensive. *Compare* 8 U.S.C. §1101(a)(33) *with* 26 U.S.C. §7701(b)(1)(A). It is unclear whether the drafters of the NDAA had either of these definitions in mind when they used the term "lawful resident alien." The 2012 NDAA is not the first instance where legislation has used the term "lawful resident alien." For example, a few legislative proposals introduced in the mid-1990s but not enacted into law used the term to refer to a particular category of aliens eligible for government benefits. *See, e.g.*, H.R. 999, the Welfare Reform and Consolidation Act of 1995 (104th Cong.); H.R. 3960, the American Health Security Act of 1994 (103rd Cong.). However, these bills defined "lawful resident aliens" differently from one another, which seems to affirm the view that the term has no generally understood meaning.

the NDAA intended the term "lawful resident alien" to also include other aliens who are lawfully present in the United States on a long-term basis but who do not have LPR status (e.g., an alien lawfully present in the United States for an extended period pursuant to a student visa).

When signing the 2012 NDAA into law, President Obama claimed that Section 1021 "breaks no new ground and is unnecessary," as it "solely codifies established authorities"[85]—namely, detention authority conferred by the AUMF, as interpreted by the Supreme Court and lower court decisions. President Obama also announced that he would "not authorize the indefinite military detention without trial of American citizens," regardless of whether such detention would be permissible under the AUMF or the 2012 NDAA.

Mandatory Military Detention

The provision that appears to have evoked the most resistance on the part of the Administration, Section 1022, generally requires at least temporary military custody for certain Al Qaeda members and members of certain "associated forces" who are taken into the custody or brought under the control of the United States as of 60 days from the date of enactment. This provision does not apply to all persons who are permitted to be detained as "covered persons" under Section 1021, but only those captured during the course of hostilities who meet certain criteria. It expressly excludes U.S. citizens from its purview, although it applies to lawful resident aliens (albeit with the caveat that if detention is based on conduct taking place within the United States, such detention is mandated only "to the extent permitted by the Constitution of the United States").[86] Moreover, the President is authorized to waive the provision's application if he submits a certification to Congress that "such a waiver is in the national security interests of the United States" (for discussion of executive's implementation of Section 1022, including its exercise of waiver authority, see *infra* at "Developments Since the Enactment of the 2012 NDAA").

The mandatory detention requirement applies to covered persons captured in the course of hostilities authorized by the AUMF, defining "covered persons" for its purposes as a person subject to detention under Section 1021 who is determined

> (A) to be a member of, or part of, al-Qaeda or an associated force that acts in coordination with or pursuant to the direction al al-Qaeda; and
>
> (B) to have participated in the course of planning or carrying out an attack or attempted attack against the United States or its coalition partners.

---

[85] Presidential Signing Statement on 2012 NDAA, *supra* footnote 4. The White House had previously expressed concern that congressional attempts to codify existing detention authorities was "unnecessary and poses some risk." *See* White House Statement on S. 1867, *supra* footnote 2, at 1-2. When S. 1867, 112th Cong., was reported out of committee, the Obama Administration expressed concern about a provision corresponding to Section 1021 in the enacted 2012 NDAA, cautioning that

> Congress must be careful not to open a whole new series of legal questions that will distract from our efforts to protect the country. While the current language minimizes many of those risks, future legislative action must ensure that the codification in statute of express military detention authority does not carry unintended consequences that could compromise our ability to protect the American people.

Id.

[86] As discussed *supra*, the term "lawful resident alien" is not defined by the 2012 NDAA or other federal statute, and there may be some ambiguity as to who falls under this category.

Persons described above are required to be detained by military authorities pending "disposition under the law of war," as defined in Section 1021, except that additional requirements must first be met before the detainee can be transferred to another country. Accordingly, such persons may be (1) held in military detention until hostilities under the AUMF are terminated; (2) tried before a military commission; (3) transferred from military custody for trial by another court having jurisdiction; or (4) transferred to the custody of a foreign government or entity, provided the transfer requirements established in Section 1028 of the act,[87] discussed *infra*, are satisfied. If the Administration wishes to prosecute a person covered by Section 1022 in a civilian trial, Section 1029 requires the Attorney General to first consult with the National Director of Intelligence and the Secretary of Defense to determine whether a military commission is more appropriate and whether the individual should be held in military custody pending trial.[88]

Section 1022 applies both to members of Al Qaeda and "associated forces."[89] The provision further specifies that covered forces are ones that "act in coordination with or pursuant to the direction of al-Qaeda." The omission of any express reference to the Taliban in Section 1022 seems to indicate that it need not be treated as a force associated with Al Qaeda, at least unless its actions are sufficiently coordinated or directed by Al Qaeda.[90] A question might arise if an associated force acts largely independently but coordinates some activity with Al Qaeda. Would all of its members be subject to mandatory detention, or only those involved in units which coordinate their activities with Al Qaeda? Perhaps this determination can be made with reference

---

[87] Section 1022 provides that persons subject to mandatory detention may be transferred to foreign countries only so long as such transfers are "consistent with the requirements of section 1028" of the bill, which bars the transfer of Guantanamo detainees to foreign countries unless certain certification requirements are met. Arguably, the interplay between these two provisions could be read to mean that no person subject to the mandatory detention requirement of Section 1022 may be transferred a foreign country unless the Secretary of Defense certifies that the transfer complies with the criteria described under Section 1028, regardless of the current location of the person's detention. The Department of Defense appears to construe the interplay of Sections 1022 and 1028 in this fashion. *See* Letter from the Secretary of Defense to Senator Carl Levin (November15, 2011) (hereinafter "DOD Letter")(discussing relationship between corresponding provisions in S. 1867), *available at* http://www.politico.com/static/ PPM229_111115_dodletter html. On the other hand, it is possible that the certification requirement is only intended to apply to those persons who are subject to mandatory detention under Section 1022 who are also currently being held at Guantanamo.

[88] The consultation requirement also applies to the trial of any other person in military detention overseas under the authority described in Section 1021, which could presumably apply to U.S. citizens.

[89] Although the final version of the 2012 NDAA uses "associated forces" (the same terminology that has been used to define detention authority in habeas litigation), an earlier version of the defense authorization bill would have applied to members of "affiliated entities." S. 1253, §1032. "Affiliated entity" does not appear to have a set definition. The recently released 2011 National Strategy for Counterterrorism (2011 Strategy), http://www.whitehouse.gov/sites/ default/files/counterterrorism_strategy.pdf distinguishes between "affiliates," which are defined as "groups that have aligned with" Al Qaeda, and "adherents," which are "individuals who have formed collaborative relationships with, act on behalf of, or are otherwise inspired to take action in furtherance of the goals of al-Qa'ida—the organization and the ideology—including by engaging in violence regardless of whether such violence is targeted at the United States, its citizens, or its interests." 2011 Strategy at 3. The 2011 Strategy also distinguishes "affiliates" from "associated forces":

> Affiliates is not a legal term of art. Although it includes Associated Forces, it additionally includes groups and individuals against whom the United States is not authorized to use force based on the authorities granted by the [AUMF]. The use of Affiliates in this strategy is intended to reflect a broader category of entities against whom the United States must bring various elements of national power, as appropriate and consistent with the law, to counter the threat they pose. Associated Forces is a legal term of art that refers to cobelligerents of al-Qa'ida or the Taliban against whom the President is authorized to use force (including the authority to detain) based on the [AUMF]. *Id.* at footnote 1.

[90] According to the conference report, the conferees agreed that the Taliban is covered by Section 1021 but not 1022. H.Rept. 112-329 at 159.

---

to the specific attack the individual is determined to have attempted, planned, or engaged. In any event, Section 1022 would not apply to a "lone wolf" terrorist with no ties to Al Qaeda or any associated force.

What conduct constitutes an "attack ... against the United States coalition partners" is not further clarified.[91] It could be read to cover only the kinds of attacks carried out in a military theater of operations against armed forces, where the law of war is generally understood to permit the military detention of such persons. This reading may be bolstered by the limitation of the provision to persons who are "captured during the course of hostilities." On the other hand, the term "attack" might be interpreted to apply more broadly to cover terrorist acts directed against civilian targets elsewhere, although the application of the law of war to such circumstances is much less certain. It is unclear whether an effort to bring down a civilian airliner, for example, necessarily constitutes an "attack against the United States." The reference to the possibility that lawful resident aliens may be detained based on conduct taking place in the United States supports the broader reading of "attack." Some proponents have suggested that the provision is intended to cover cases such as that of Umar Farouk Abdulmutallab,[92] the Nigerian suspect accused of trying to destroy an airliner traveling from Amsterdam to Detroit on Christmas Day 2009, although he was arrested by domestic law enforcement authorities, which suggests that the bill is intended to consider future similar occurrences as "attacks against the United States" that involve captures during the "course of hostilities."

In response to Administration objections to the mandatory detention provision originally found in S. 1253, 112th Congress, a new requirement was established in S. 1867, 112th Congress, which was ultimately included in the enacted version of the 2012 NDAA, that the President must submit to Congress, within 60 days of enactment, a report describing the procedures for implementing the mandatory detention provision. The procedural requirements were added to respond to criticism that the measure would interfere with law enforcement and interrogation efforts, among other perceived risks. The submission was required to include procedures for designating who is authorized to determine who is a covered person for the purpose of the provision and the process by which such determinations are to be made. Other procedures to be described include those for preventing the interruption of ongoing surveillance or intelligence gathering with regard to persons not already in the custody or control of the United States; precluding implementation of the determination process until after any ongoing interrogation session is completed and precluding the interruption of an interrogation session; precluding application of the provision in the case of an individual who remains in the custody of a third country, where U.S. government officials are permitted access to the individual; and providing for an exercise of waiver authority to accomplish the transfer of a covered person from a third country, if necessary. This requirement applies only to persons taken into custody on or after the 2012 NDAA's date of enactment.

---

[91] The presidential policy directive announcing procedures implementing Section 1022 defines an "attack" as "an act of violence or the use of force that involves serious risk to human life," with no further specification as to whether such an act must occur in a military theater of operations. Presidential Directive on Section 1022, *supra* footnote 5, at 2. However, it limits the scope of application of the procedures for implementing Section 1022 to persons arrested or otherwise taken into custody by the FBI or other law enforcement agencies, *id.*, suggesting that a broader interpretation of "attack" may have been adopted.

[92] *See, e.g.*, 157 Cong. Rec. S8097 (daily ed. December 1, 2011) (statement of Sen. Ayotte). *See also* White House Statement on S. 1867, *supra* footnote 2, at 2 ("Moreover, applying this military custody requirement to individuals inside the United States, as some Members of Congress have suggested is their intention, would raise serious and unsettled legal questions and would be inconsistent with the fundamental American principle that our military does not patrol our streets.").

It is not clear how these procedures will interact with those contemplated under Section 1024 (discussed more fully *infra*), which requires DOD to submit to Congress procedures for status determinations for persons detained pursuant to the AUMF for purposes of Section 1021. If the procedures required by Section 1022 are meant to determine whether a person is detainable under the AUMF (per Section 1021) as an initial matter (as opposed to determining the appropriate disposition under the law of war), then it would seem necessary for that determination to take place prior to the procedures for determining whether a person's detention is *required* under Section 1022.[93] The act does not appear to preclude the implementation of more than one process for making the determination that someone qualifies as a covered person subject to mandatory military detention, perhaps depending on whether the person is initially in military custody or the custody of law enforcement officials. Nor does it seem to preclude the use of a single procedure to determine whether a person is covered by Section 1022 *and* the appropriate disposition under the law of war, which could obviate the necessity for transferring a person to military custody. Whatever process is adopted to make any of these determinations would likely implicate constitutional due process requirements, at least if the detainee is located within the United States or is a U.S. citizen, and would likely be subject to challenge by means of habeas corpus.[94] Section 1022 does not prevent Article III trials of covered persons,[95] although any time spent in military custody could complicate the prosecution of a covered defendant.[96]

The Obama Administration opposed this provision, even as the language was revised.[97] During Senate deliberation concerning S. 1867, 112th Congress, the White House claimed that its mandatory military detention requirement constituted an "unnecessary, untested, and legally

---

[93] If the Administration concludes that existing law and authority with respect to persons arrested within the United States does not support their treatment as persons detainable under the AUMF as described under Section 1021, it may be able to avoid determining whether any who are non-U.S. citizens are subject to the provisions of Section 1022.

[94] The ability of a detainee to bring a habeas petition under Section 1036 may depend upon his location. *Compare* Boumediene v. Bush, 553 U.S. 723 (2008) (constitutional writ of habeas extends to non-citizen detainees held at Guantanamo) *with* Maqaleh v. Gates, 605 F.3d 84 (D.C. Cir. 2010) (writ of habeas does not presently extend to non-citizen detainees held by the United States in Afghanistan).

[95] No funds authorized to be appropriated under the 2012 NDAA were permitted to be used to transfer detainees to the United States from Guantanamo for trial. Subsequent appropriations and authorization enactments effectively extended the bar on detainee transfers through FY2013. *See* FY2013 Consolidated and Full Year Continuing Appropriations Act, P.L. 113-6, Div. B, §530 and Div. C., §8109; 2013 NDAA, P.L. 112-239, §1027.

[96] There has been one case of an individual who was transferred from Guantanamo to the United States for prosecution on terrorism charges. Ahmed Khalfan Ghailani was indicted in 1998 and charged with conspiracy in connection with the bombing of the United States Embassies in Nairobi, Kenya, and Dar es Salaam, Tanzania. He was arrested in Pakistan in 2004 and turned over to U.S. custody to be held and interrogated by Central Intelligence Agency (CIA) officials. In 2006, he was transferred to DOD custody and held as an enemy combatant at Guantanamo. He was transferred to the Southern District of New York for trial in 2009, and was subsequently convicted and sentenced to life imprisonment, despite his efforts to quash the prosecution on numerous grounds related to his detention. For more information, see CRS Report R41156, *Judicial Activity Concerning Enemy Combatant Detainees: Major Court Rulings*, by Jennifer K. Elsea and Michael John Garcia.

[97] For example, during Senate consideration of S. 1867, 112th Cong., Secretary of Defense Panetta expressed doubt that its mandatory military detention provision offered any advantage to DOD or to U.S. national security interests, predicting instead that it would restrain the executive branch's option to make effective use of all available counterterrorism tools. Moreover, Secretary Panetta objected to the provision's failure to clearly limit its scope to persons captured abroad; complained that the qualification to "associated force" (limiting mandatory detention to members of such groups that coordinate with or act under the direction of Al Qaeda) unnecessarily complicates the Department's ability to interpret and implement the restriction; and viewed as inappropriate the possible extension of the transfer certification requirements of Section 1033 (now Section 1028) to those covered by Section 1032 (now Section 1022) who are not currently detained at Guantanamo. *See* DOD Letter, *supra* footnote 87.

controversial restriction of the President's authority to defend the Nation from terrorist threats" that would "tie the hands of our intelligence and law enforcement professionals."[98]

However, a new proviso was added in conference, which, along with a shift of waiver authority from the Secretary of Defense to the President, apparently reduced Administration concerns to the extent necessary to avert a veto.[99] Section 1022, as it emerged from conference, provides that it is not to be construed "to affect the existing criminal enforcement and national security authorities of the Federal Bureau of Investigation or any other domestic law enforcement agency with regard to a covered person, regardless whether such covered person is held in military custody." While FBI Director Robert Mueller expressed concern that the provision, even as revised in conference, could create confusion as to the FBI's role in responding to a terrorist attack,[100] the White House issued a statement explaining that, as a result of changes made in conference (as well as some that had been made prior to Senate passage): "[W]e have concluded that the language does not challenge or constrain the President's ability to collect intelligence, incapacitate dangerous terrorists, and protect the American people, and the President's senior advisors will not recommend a veto."[101]

However, the statement also warned that "if in the process of implementing this law we determine that it will negatively impact our counterterrorism professionals and undercut our commitment to the rule of law, we expect that the authors of these provisions will work quickly and tirelessly to correct these problems."[102]

When signing the 2012 NDAA into law, President Obama expressed strong disapproval of Section 1022, describing it as "ill-conceived and ... [doing] nothing to improve the security of the United States."[103] Nonetheless, the President characterized the Section 1022 as providing "the minimally acceptable amount of flexibility to protect national security," and claimed that he would interpret and apply it so as to best preserve executive discretion when determining the appropriate means for dealing with a suspected terrorist in U.S. custody:

> Specifically, I have signed this bill on the understanding that section 1022 provides the executive branch with broad authority to determine how best to implement it, and with the full and unencumbered ability to waive any military custody requirement, including the option of waiving appropriate categories of cases when doing so is in the national security interests of the United States. As my Administration has made clear, the only responsible way to combat the threat al-Qa'ida poses is to remain relentlessly practical, guided by the factual and legal complexities of each case and the relative strengths and weaknesses of each system. Otherwise, investigations could be compromised, our authorities to hold dangerous individuals could be jeopardized, and intelligence could be lost. I will not tolerate that result, and under no circumstances will my Administration accept or adhere to a rigid across-the-board requirement for military detention. I will therefore interpret and implement section

---

[98] *See* White House Statement on S. 1867, *supra* footnote 2, at 2.

[99] White House Press Briefing by Press Secretary Jay Carney, December 15, 2011, *available at* http://www.whitehouse.gov/the-press-office/2011/12/15/press-briefing-press-secretary-jay-carney-12152011.

[100] *See* FBI Oversight, Hearing before the Senate Committee on the Judiciary, 112th Cong. 2d Sess. (December 14, 2011)(Statement of FBI Director Robert Mueller), *transcript available at* 2011 WL 6202873.

[101] Statement from the White House Press Secretary on the NDAA Bill, December 14, 2011, printed in National Defense Authorization Act for Fiscal Year 2012—Conference Report, 157 CONG. REC. S8632-01, S8664 (2011).

[102] *Id.*

[103] Presidential Signing Statement on 2012 NDAA, *supra* footnote 4.

1022 in the manner that best preserves the same flexible approach that has served us so well for the past 3 years and that protects the ability of law enforcement professionals to obtain the evidence and cooperation they need to protect the Nation.[104]

On February 28, 2012, President Obama issued a directive concerning the implementation of Section 1022, and announcing circumstances in which the mandatory detention requirements would be waived. This directive is discussed in more detail *infra* at "Developments Since the Enactment of the 2012 NDAA."

Periodic Review of Detention of Persons at Guantanamo

Section 1023 addresses Executive Order 13567, pertaining to detention reviews at Guantanamo. Unlike H.R. 1540, as originally passed by the House of Representatives of the 112th Congress,[105] the corresponding Senate provision incorporated into the enacted 2012 NDAA does not seek to replace the periodic review process established by the order, as a corresponding House provision would have done,[106] but instead seeks to clarify aspects of the process. Section 1023 requires the Secretary of Defense, within 180 days of enactment, to submit to the congressional defense and intelligence committees a report setting forth procedures to be employed by review panels established pursuant to Executive Order 13567. The provision requires that these new review procedures to

- clarify that the purpose of the periodic review is not to review the legality of any particular detention, but to determine whether a detainee poses a continuing threat to U.S. security;

- clarify that the Secretary of Defense, after considering the results and recommendations of a reviewing panel, is responsible for any final decision to release or transfer a detainee and is not bound by the recommendations; and

- ensure that appropriate consideration is given to a list of factors, including the likelihood the detainee will resume terrorist activity or rejoin a group engaged in hostilities against the United States; the likelihood of family, tribal, or

---

[104] *Id.*

[105] Among other things, the review process contemplated by Section 1036 of H.R. 1540, as initially passed by the House during the 112th Congress, would have required that the initial review panel consist of military officers rather than senior officials from multiple agencies; imposed more detailed and stringent criteria for assessing whether an individual's continued detention is no longer warranted; and limited the assistance private counsel may provide to detainees. Section 1036 also would have required the establishment of an interagency review board, composed of senior officials of the Department of State, the Department of Defense, the Department of Justice, the Department of Homeland Security, the Joint Chiefs of Staff, and the Office of the Director of National Intelligence. The interagency review board was to be responsible for reviewing the military panel's review for clear error. In a written statement regarding H.R. 1540, the White House identified Section 1036 as one of several provisions within the bill that might contribute to a decision to veto. It asserted that the periodic review process established by Section 1036

> undermines the system of periodic review established by the President's ... Executive Order by substituting a rigid system of review that could limit the advice and expertise of critical intelligence and law enforcement professionals, undermining the Executive branch's ability to ensure that these decisions are informed by all available information and protect the full spectrum of our national security interests. It also unnecessarily interferes with DOD's ability to manage detention operations.

White House Statement on H.R. 1540, *supra* footnote 2, at 2-3.

[106] H.R. 1540 (as initially passed by the House, 112th Cong.) §1036.

---

government rehabilitation or support for the detainee; the likelihood the detainee may be subject to trial by military commission; and any law enforcement interest in the detainee.

The Administration had objected to this provision because it said it would shift to the Defense Department the responsibility for what had been a collaborative, interagency review process.[107] The provision was modified in conference to clarify that the procedures apply to "any individual who is detained as an unprivileged enemy belligerent at Guantanamo at any time on or after the date of enactment" of the act.

The conference report for the 2012 NDAA explains that the conferees understood that the review process

> established by the Executive Order is not a legal proceeding and does not create any discovery rights in the detainee, his personal representative, or private counsel. For this reason, the conferees expect the procedures established under this section to provide that: (1) the compilation of information for the review process should be conducted in good faith, but does not create any rights on behalf of the detainee; (2) the mitigating information to be provided to the detainee is information compiled in the course of this good faith compilation effort; (3) the decision whether to permit the calling of witnesses and the presentation of statements by persons other than the detainee is discretionary, and not a matter of right; and (4) access to classified information on the part of private counsel is subject to national security constraints, clearance requirements, and the availability of resources to review and clear relevant information.

In a statement issued upon signing the 2012 NDAA into law, President Obama characterized this provision as "needlessly interfere[ing] with the executive branch's processes for reviewing the status of detainees."[108]

Status Determination of Wartime Detainees

Section 1024 of the 2012 NDAA, which tracks a provision contained in S. 1867, 112th Congress, requires the Secretary of Defense, within 90 days of enactment, to submit a report to congressional defense and intelligence committees explaining the procedures for determining the status of persons detained under the AUMF for purposes of Section 1021 of the Senate bill. It is not clear whether the status determination "for purposes of section 1021" means determination of whether a detained individual is a "covered person" subject to Section 1021, or whether it is meant to refer to the disposition of such a person under the law of war, or to both.[109]

---

[107] White House Statement on S. 1867, *supra* footnote 2, at 2.

[108] Presidential Signing Statement on 2012 NDAA, *supra* footnote 4.

[109] The language of Section 1024 largely mirrors that originally found in Section 1036 of S. 1253. The revised language omits reference to "unprivileged enemy belligerent" to modify "status" in the heading, but this alteration does not appear to affect the meaning of the provision itself. The original version applied to persons captured in the course of hostilities authorized by the AUMF rather than those detained pursuant to it, which seemed to indicate that it was meant to be an initial status determination only for those newly captured. On the other hand, explanatory language in the conference report described the Senate provision, Section 1036, as requiring the Secretary of Defense "to establish procedures for determining the status of *persons captured in the course of hostilities* authorized by [the AUMF]," H.Rept. 112-329 at 160 (emphasis added), which suggests that conferees did not attach much significance to the phrase "captured in the course of hostilities" as a limitation on the provision's coverage.

In the case of any unprivileged enemy belligerent who will be held in long-term detention, clause (b) of the provision requires the procedures to provide the following elements:

> (1) A military judge shall preside at proceedings for the determination of status of an unprivileged enemy belligerent.
>
> (2) An unprivileged enemy belligerent may, at the election of the belligerent, be represented by military counsel at proceedings for the determination of status of the belligerent.

The requirements of this provision apply without regard to the location where the detainee is held. It would appear to afford detainees held by the United States in Afghanistan greater privileges during status determination hearings than they may have earlier possessed (at least in circumstances where the United States intends to place them in "long-term detention," in which case the requirements of Section 1024(b) are triggered).[110] It is not clear what effect this provision would have upon detainees currently held at Guantanamo, who were designated as "enemy combatants" subject to military detention using a status review process that did not fully comply with the requirements of Section 1024(b).[111] The version of Section 1024 reported out of conference modified the provision to explain that the procedures applicable in the case of long-term detention need not apply to persons for whom habeas corpus review is available in federal court, which suggests it does not apply to Guantanamo detainees. According to the explanatory material in the conference report, the Secretary of Defense is authorized to determine what constitutes "long-term detention" as well as the "the extent, if any, to which such procedures will be applied to detainees for whom status determinations have already been made prior to" the date of enactment.

The provision does not explain, in the case of new captures, how it is to be determined prior to the status hearing whether a detainee is one who will be held in long-term detention and whose hearing is thus subject to special requirements, but "long-term detention" could be interpreted with reference to law of war principles to refer to enemy belligerents held for the duration of hostilities to prevent their return to combat, a permissible "disposition under the law of war" under Sections 1021 and 1022 of the bill.[112] This reading, however, suggests that the disposition determination is to be made prior to a status determination, which seems counterintuitive, or that a second status determination is required for those designated for long-term detention. Explanatory material in the conference report indicates that the long-term procedures might not be triggered by an initial review after capture, but might be triggered by subsequent reviews, at the discretion of the Secretary of Defense. This remark suggests that both the initial determination that a person may be detained as well as any subsequent process for determining the appropriate disposition of the detainee are meant to be covered, but that the requirement for additional rights for long-term detainees may apply only in limited circumstances.[113] Captured unprivileged enemy belligerents destined for trial by military commission or Article III court, or to be transferred to a foreign country or entity, would not appear to be entitled to be represented by military counsel or to have a military judge preside at their status determination proceedings.

---

[110] *See supra* citations contained in footnote 51.

[111] *See supra* section headed "Status Determinations for Unprivileged Enemy Belligerents."

[112] Unlike the corresponding provision in S. 1253, Section 1031 of S. 1867 did not use "long-term" to modify "detention under the law of war."

[113] H.Rept. 112-329 at 160.

The White House expressed disapproval of this provision. Prior to enactment, the Obama Administration claimed that the provision would establish "onerous requirements [and] conflict[] with procedures for detainee reviews in the field that have been developed based on many years of experience by military officers and the Department of Defense."[114] When signing the 2012 NDAA into law, President Obama declared that, "consistent with congressional intent as detailed in the Conference Report," the executive branch would "interpret section 1024 as granting the Secretary of Defense broad discretion to determine what detainee status determinations in Afghanistan are subject to the requirements of this section."[115]

Security Protocols for Guantanamo Detainees

Section 1025 contains a modified requirement that originated as Section 1035 in the House bill, which would have required the Secretary of Defense to submit a detailed "national security protocol" pertaining to the communications of each individual detained at Guantanamo within 90 days of enactment. The conference report amended the provision to require a single protocol, to be submitted within 180 days, covering the policy and procedures applicable to all detainees at Guantanamo. The protocol is required to describe an array of limitations or privileges applicable to detainees regarding access to military or civilian legal representation, communications with counsel or any other person, receipt of information, possession of contraband and the like, as well as applicable enforcement measures. The provision specifically requires a description of monitoring procedures for legal materials or communications for the protection of national security while also preserving the detainee's privilege to protect such materials and communications in connection with a military commission trial or habeas proceeding. In President Obama's signing statement for the 2012 NDAA, he characterized this provision as needlessly interfering with executive branch processes for reviewing the status of detainees.[116]

Transfer or Release of Wartime Detainees into the United States

While not directly limiting the transfer or release of detainees into the United States, Section 1026 prohibited the use of any funds made available to the Department of Defense for FY2012 to construct or modify any facility in the United States, its territories, or possessions to house an individual detained at Guantanamo for "detention or imprisonment in the custody or under the control of the Department of Defense." Substantially similar restrictions have been contained in subsequent appropriations and authorization legislation, including the 2014 NDAA and the 2014 Omnibus.[117]

Section 1027 prohibited the expenditure of DOD funds for FY2012 from being used to transfer or assist in the transfer of detainees from Guantanamo into the United States. It was derived from a much broader restriction in Section 1039 of the House bill, which would have limited the transfer or release into the United States of any non-citizen detainees held abroad in U.S. military custody.[118]

---

[114] White House Statement on S. 1867, *supra* footnote 2, at 3.

[115] Presidential Signing Statement on 2012 NDAA, *supra* footnote 4.

[116] *Id.*

[117] 2014 NDAA, P.L. 113-66, §1033; 2014 Omnibus, P.L. 113-76, Div. B, §528, Div. C, §8112, and Div. J, §412.

[118] The restriction also generally precludes the transfer or release of detainees to U.S. territories or possessions.

Section 1027 is a continuation of transfer restrictions from prior legislation. In response to the Obama Administration's stated plan to close the Guantanamo detention facility and transfer at least some detainees into the United States, Congress has enacted several funding measures in recent years intended to limit executive discretion to transfer or release Guantanamo detainees into the United States. Initially, these measures barred detainees from being released into the United States, but still preserved executive discretion to transfer detainees into the country for purposes of criminal prosecution.[119] However, more recent funding limitations, including those contained in the 2012 Minibus and the 2012 CAA, prohibited the transfer of Guantanamo detainees into the United States for any purpose, including criminal prosecution.[120] This version of the restriction was extended until the end of FY2013 by the 2013 NDAA,[121] and then through the end of FY2014 by the 2014 NDAA and the 2014 Omnibus.[122] The measures appear to have been motivated in part by the Administration's plans to transfer Khalid Sheik Mohammed and several other Guantanamo detainees to the United States to stand trial in an Article III court. As no civilian court operates at Guantanamo, the legislation appears to have effectively made military commissions the only viable forum for the criminal prosecution of Guantanamo detainees, at least until the end of FY2014.

During congressional deliberations over H.R. 1540, as originally passed by the House during the 112th Congress, the Obama Administration issued a statement expressing opposition to the provision in the bill which barred the transfer of detainees into the United States.[123] While stating its opposition to the release of detainees into the United States, the Obama Administration claimed that the measure would unduly interfere with executive discretion to prosecute detainees in an Article III court located in the United States. According to a White House statement, the restriction on any detainee transfers into the country would be

> a dangerous and unprecedented challenge to critical Executive branch authority to determine when and where to prosecute detainees, based on the facts and the circumstances of each case and our national security interests. It unnecessarily constrains our Nation's counterterrorism efforts and would undermine our national security, particularly where our Federal courts are the best—or even the only—option for incapacitating dangerous terrorists.[124]

The modification in conference to encompass only Guantanamo detainees, as previous legislation had already done, rather than to all detainees in military custody abroad was apparently sufficient

---

[119] For further discussion of these limitations, see CRS Report R40754, *Guantanamo Detention Center: Legislative Activity in the 111ᵗʰ Congress*, by Michael John Garcia.

[120] 2012 Minibus, P.L. 112-55, §532; 2012 CAA, P.L. 112-74, §§511, 8119. *See also* 2011 NDAA, P.L. 111-383, §1032 (expired at the end of FY2011); 2011 CAA, P.L. 112-10, §1112 (extended beyond FY2011 and through December 16, 2011, via Division D of the 2012 Minibus).

[121] 2013 NDAA, P.L. 112-239, §1027; FY2013 Consolidated and Full Year Continuing Appropriations Act, P.L. 113-6, Div. B, §530 and Div. C., §8109.

[122] 2014 NDAA, P.L. 113-66, §1034; 2014 Omnibus, P.L. 113-76, Div. B., §528, Div. C, §8110, and Div. G, §537.

[123] Upon signing the 2011 NDAA and CAA into law, which each imposed blanket restrictions on the transfer or release of Guantanamo detainees into the United States, President Obama issued statements expressing his disapproval of the restrictions they imposed upon executive discretion to bring detainees into the country for trial before an Article III court. White House Office of the Press Secretary, Statement by the President on H.R. 6523, January 7, 2011, *available at* http://www.whitehouse.gov/the-press-office/2011/01/07/statement-president-hr-6523; White House Office of the Press Secretary, Statement by the President on H.R. 1473, April 15, 2011, *available at* http://www.whitehouse.gov/the-press-office/2011/04/15/statement-president-hr-1473.

[124] White House Statement on H.R. 1540, *supra* footnote 2, at 2.

to overcome the veto threat. Nonetheless, President Obama stated when signing the 2012 NDAA that he remained opposed to the provision, as it intrudes upon "critical executive branch authority to determine when and where to prosecute Guantanamo detainees."[125] He also asserted that the provision could, "under certain circumstances, violate constitutional separation of powers principles," but did not specify a situation where such a conflict may arise. He further claimed that when Section 1027 would operate in a manner violating separation of powers principle, his Administration would interpret the provision to avoid a constitutional conflict.

Transfer or Release of Guantanamo Detainees to Foreign Countries

Section 1028 limited funds made available to DOD for the 2012 fiscal year from being used to transfer or release Guantanamo detainees to foreign countries or entities, except when certain criteria were met. These limitations did not apply in cases where a Guantanamo detainee is transferred or released to effectuate a court order (i.e., when a habeas court finds that a detainee is not subject to detention under the AUMF and orders the government to effectuate his release from custody). The restrictions established by Section 1028 largely mirrored those contained in the 2012 CAA,[126] both of which remained in effect for the duration of the 2012 fiscal year (and which were effectively extended by continuing resolution until March 27, 2013, by the 2013 CAR,[127] and until the end of FY2013 by the 2013 NDAA and the FY2013 Consolidated and Full Year Continuing Appropriations Act[128]), as well as those restrictions which were contained in the Ike Skelton National Defense Authorization Act for FY2011 (2011 NDAA; P.L. 111-383) and the Department of Defense and Full-Year Continuing Appropriations Act, 2011 (2011 CAA; P.L. 112-10), which had been set to expire at the end of FY2011.[129] Congressional notification requirements relating to detainee transfers which were subsequently established by the Intelligence Authorization Act for FY2012 (P.L. 112-87) did not modify existing legislative restrictions on transfers from Guantanamo.[130]

Restrictions on Guantanamo detainee transfers appear motivated by congressional concern over possible recidivism by persons released from U.S. custody.[131] Supporters of these funding restrictions argue that they significantly reduce the chance that a detainee will reengage in terrorist activity if released, while critics argue that they are overly stringent and hamper the executive's ability to transfer even low-risk detainees from U.S. custody. In any event, detainee

---

[125] Presidential Signing Statement on 2012 NDAA, *supra* footnote 4.

[126] 2012 CAA, P.L. 112-74, §8120.

[127] Continuing Appropriations Resolution, 2013 (P.L. 112-175) (generally extending funding restrictions imposed by 2012 CAA or 2012 Minibus until March 27, 2013).

[128] P.L. 112-239, §1028; FY2013 Consolidated and Full Year Continuing Appropriations Act, P.L. 113-6, Div. C., §8110.

[129] Most of the applicable restrictions on detainee transfers contained in the 2011 NDAA and CAA concern funds made available for FY2011 (which ended on September 30, 2011). However, the 2011 NDAA's prohibition on the transfer of detainees to any country where there has been a confirmed case of recidivism by a previously transferred detainee expired in January 2012. 2011 NDAA, P.L. 111-383, §1333(c) (specifying that prohibition lasts for a one-year period beginning on the date of enactment). The restrictions contained in the 2011 CAA were temporarily extended via continuing resolution beyond the 2011 fiscal year. 2012 Minibus, P.L. 112-55, Div. D (generally extended funding for federal agencies pursuant to the terms and conditions of the 2011 CAA through December 16, 2011).

[130] Intelligence Authorization Act for FY2012, P.L. 112-87, §308 (requiring congressional notification 30 days before a Guantanamo detainee may be transferred or released to a foreign country, and specifying that this requirement does not modify transfer restrictions established by the 2012 NDAA).

[131] *See supra*, discussion at ""Recidivism" and Restrictions on Transfer."

---

transfers became far more infrequent after the 2011 NDAA and CAA went into effect, though the degree to which these restrictions are responsible for the lack of subsequent detainee transfers is unclear.

Under the requirements of Section 1028, in order for a transfer to occur, the Secretary of Defense was required to first certify to Congress that the destination country or entity

- was not presently a designated state sponsor of terrorism or terrorist organization;

- maintained control over each detention facility where a transferred detainee may have been housed;

- was not presently facing a threat likely to substantially affect its ability to control a transferred detainee;

- agreed to take effective steps to ensure that the transferred person did not pose a future threat to the United States, its citizens, or its allies;

- agreed to take such steps as the Secretary deemed necessary to prevent the detainee from engaging in terrorism; and

- agreed to share relevant information with the United States related to the transferred detainee that may affect the security of the United States, its citizens, or its allies.

These certification requirements virtually mirror those contained in the 2011 NDAA and CAA.[132] A House provision that would have established an additional requirement that the receiving foreign entity agree to permit U.S. authorities to have access to the transferred individual was not included in the conference report.

Section 1028 also generally prohibited transfers from Guantanamo to any foreign country or entity if there was a confirmed case of a detainee previously transferred to that place or entity who has subsequently engaged in any terrorist activity. The prohibition did not apply in the case of detainees who were to be transferred pursuant to either a pretrial agreement in a military commission case, if entered prior to the enactment, or a court order.

Both the certification requirement and the bar related to recidivism could be waived if the Secretary of Defense determined, with the concurrence of the Secretary of State and in consultation with the Director of National Intelligence, that alternative actions would be taken to address the underlying purpose of the measures, or that, in the event that agreements or actions on the part of the receiving state or entity could not be certified as eliminating all relevant risks, alternative actions would substantially mitigate the risk.[133] In the case of a waiver of the provision barring transfers anywhere recidivism has occurred, the Secretary was permitted to issue a waiver if alternative actions would be taken to mitigate the risk of recidivism. Any transfer pursuant to a waiver was required to first be determined to be in the national security interests of the United

---

[132] 2011 NDAA, P.L. 111-383, §1033; 2011 CAA, P.L. 112-10, §1013.

[133] While the funding restrictions on detainee transfers contained in the 2011 NDAA and CAA afforded the Secretary of Defense limited waiver authority, they did not permit the waiver of certification requirements. Moreover, although the Section 1028 permits the Secretary to waive the prohibition on the transfer of detainees where there is a confirmed case of recidivism, it establishes more stringent requirements for the exercise of this authority than the 2011 NDAA or CAA. *See* 2011 NDAA, P.L. 111-383, §1033; 2011 CAA, P.L. 112-10, §1113.

States. Not later than 30 days prior to the transfer, copies of the determination and the waiver were required to be submitted to the congressional defense committees, together with a statement of the basis for regarding the transfer as serving national security interests; an explanation why it was not possible to certify that all risks have been eliminated (if applicable); and a summary of the alternative actions contemplated.

The transfer restrictions in Section 1028 generally applied to any "individual detained at Guantanamo," other than a U.S. citizen or servicemember;[134] a detainee transferred pursuant to a court order; or a detainee transferred pursuant to a military commission pretrial agreement entered prior to the 2012 NDAA's enactment. This term appeared broad enough in scope to cover foreign refugees brought to the Migrant Operations Center at Guantanamo after being interdicted at sea while attempting to reach U.S. shores. Whether similarly worded provisions in successive legislation would be interpreted so broadly as to cover such persons remains to be seen. The "requirements" of the section also applied to persons subject to mandatory detention under Section 1022, but not to all "covered persons" within the meaning of Section 1021 (who are not detained at Guantanamo).[135]

During congressional deliberations over the House and Senate bills competing to become the 2012 NDAA, the White House and DOD expressed disapproval of the transfer certification requirements contained in each bill.[136] In a statement made upon signing the 2012 NDAA into law, President Obama stated that Section 1028

> modifies but fundamentally maintains unwarranted restrictions on the executive branch's authority to transfer detainees to a foreign country. This hinders the executive's ability to carry out its military, national security, and foreign relations activities and like section 1027 [concerning detainee transfers into the United States], would, under certain circumstances, violate constitutional separation of powers principles. The executive branch must have the flexibility to act swiftly in conducting negotiations with foreign countries regarding the circumstances of detainee transfers. In the event that the statutory restrictions in sections 1027 and 1028 operate in a manner that violates constitutional separation of powers principles, my Administration will interpret them to avoid the constitutional conflict.[137]

As discussed *infra*, the restrictions imposed on detainee transfers imposed by the 2012 NDAA (and extended by the 2013 NDAA) were somewhat relaxed by the 2014 NDAA.[138]

---

[134] Section 1028(e)(2) defines "individual detained at Guantanamo" to exclude U.S. citizens and servicemembers from its scope.

[135] *See supra* section describing §1022 ("Mandatory Military Detention").

[136] The White House expressed disapproval of the restrictions on detainee transfers established by Section 1040 of the bill initially passed by the House, claiming that the provision's certification requirements unduly interfere with the executive's ability

> to make important foreign policy and national security determinations regarding whether and under what circumstances such transfers should occur. The Administration must have the ability to act swiftly and to have broad flexibility in conducting its negotiations with foreign countries. White House Statement on H.R. 1540, *supra* footnote 2, at 2.

The Department of Defense likewise disapproved of the certification provision in S. 1867, although the Secretary expressed gratitude that the provision was not made permanent (as in S. 1253). *See* DOD Letter, *supra* footnote 97.

[137] Presidential Signing Statement on 2012 NDAA, *supra* footnote 4.

[138] *See infra*, discussion at "FY2014 NDAA Detainee Provisions."

Consultation Requirement Regarding Terrorism Trials

Section 1029, which originated as Section 1042 of the House bill and has not appeared in prior legislation, requires consultation among the Attorney General, Deputy Attorney General, or Assistant Attorney General for the Criminal Division, and the Director of National Intelligence and the Secretary of Defense prior to the initiation of any prosecution in certain cases. The original provision applied to the trial of any non-citizen for an offense for which the defendant could be tried by military commission. The version that emerged from conference applies only to persons covered by the mandatory detention requirement in Section 1022 and any other person held in military detention pursuant to authority affirmed by Section 1021. As amended in conference, the consultation requirement does not apply to persons arrested in the United States unless they are non-citizens who meet the criteria for mandatory detention. However, it does seem to apply to any case of a U.S. citizen who may be detained abroad pursuant to the AUMF authority affirmed in Section 1021.

The consultation is to involve a discussion of whether the prosecution should take place in a U.S. district court or before a military commission, and whether the individual should be transferred into military custody for purposes of intelligence interviews. The White House expressed opposition to this provision in its original form, claiming that robust interagency coordination already exists between federal agencies in terrorism-related prosecutions, and asserting that the provision "would undermine, rather than enhance, this coordination by requiring institutions to assume unfamiliar roles and could cause delays in taking into custody individuals who pose imminent threats to the nation's safety."[139]

When signing the 2012 NDAA into law, President Obama claimed that Section 1029

> represents an intrusion into the functions and prerogatives of the Department of Justice and offends the longstanding legal tradition that decisions regarding criminal prosecutions should be vested with the Attorney General free from outside interference. Moreover, section 1029 could impede flexibility and hinder exigent operational judgments in a manner that damages our security. My Administration will interpret and implement section 1029 in a manner that preserves the operational flexibility of our counterterrorism and law enforcement professionals, limits delays in the investigative process, ensures that critical executive branch functions are not inhibited, and preserves the integrity and independence of the Department of Justice.[140]

Military Commissions Act Revision

Section 1030 amends the Military Commissions Act of 2009 (MCA) to expressly permit guilty pleas in capital cases brought before military commissions, so long as military commission panel members vote unanimously to approve the sentence.[141] As previously written, the MCA clearly permits the death penalty only in cases where all military commission members present vote to convict and concur in the sentence of death. This requirement had been interpreted by many as precluding the imposition of the death penalty in cases where the accused has pleaded guilty, as there would have been no vote by commission members as to the defendant's guilt. Section 1033

---

[139] White House Statement on H.R. 1540, *supra* footnote 2, at 3.

[140] Presidential Signing Statement on 2012 NDAA, *supra* footnote 4.

[141] 2012 NDAA, P.L. 112-81, H.R. 1540, §1034 (amending 10 U.S.C. §949m(b)).

also amends the MCA to address pre-trial agreements, specifically permitting such agreements to allow for a reduction in the maximum sentence, but not to permit a sentence of death to be imposed by a military judge alone.[142]

Section 1034 contains several technical amendments to the MCA that were inserted into the Senate version of the FY2012 Act prior to conference. The first change amends 10 U.S.C. Section 949A(b)(2)(c) to provide that the right to representation by counsel attaches at the time at which charges are "sworn" rather than "preferred." Several changes amend the language describing the composition of the Court of Military Commission Review to clarify that the judges on the court need not remain sitting appellate judges on another military appellate court to remain qualified to serve on the Court of Military Commission Review. Another change clarifies that the review authority of the U.S. Court of Appeals for the D.C. Circuit is limited to determinations of matters of law, apparently to resolve ambiguity in 10 U.S.C. Section 950G., which designates the appellate court for the D.C. Circuit as having exclusive jurisdiction to review final military commission judgments and defines the scope and nature of such review.[143] A final change modifies language in the same section describing the deadline for seeking review at the appellate court, apparently in order to clarify an ambiguity which suggested that only the accused (and not the government) could petition for review.

General Counterterrorism Matters

Section 1032 of the 2012 NDAA, derived from Section 1045 of the House bill, addresses the perceived need for improved interagency strategic planning for measures to deny safe havens to Al Qaeda and affiliated groups and to strengthen "at-risk states." It requires the President to issue planning guidance identifying and analyzing geographic areas of concern and to provide a set of goals for each area and a description of various agency roles as well as gaps in U.S. capabilities that may have to be filled through coordination with other entities. The provision also requires agencies involved in carrying out the guidance to enter into a memorandum of understanding covering a list of criteria. Although a requirement to submit copies of each new or updated guidance document to Congress within 15 days after its issuance was dropped in conference, the conferees noted their expectation to be briefed on the guidance.[144]

Section 1033 extends for two years the authority to make rewards up to $5 million to individuals who provide information or non-lethal assistance to the U.S. government or an ally in connection with a military operation outside the United States against international terrorism or to assist with force protection.[145] The original authority expired on September 30, 2011, but has been extended until September 30, 2014.[146] The provision also moves the related annual reporting requirement to February rather than December. The provision, which originated as Section 1034 of the House bill, was amended in conference to modify the annual reporting requirement, adding a description of program implementation for each geographic combatant command, a description of efforts to

---

[142] *Id.* (amending 10 U.S.C. §949i).

[143] The Supreme Court may review by writ of certiorari a final judgment by the D.C. Circuit Court of Appeals. 10 U.S.C. §950G(e).

[144] H.Rept. 112-329 at 163.

[145] 10 U.S.C. §127b.

[146] 2014 NDAA, P.L. 113-66, §1021.

"de-conflict the authority" to make such awards with similar U.S. government rewards programs, and an "assessment of the effectiveness of the program in meeting its objectives."

Developments Since the Enactment of the 2012 NDAA

The Department of Defense has published guidelines for the implementation of the periodic review process established for Guantanamo detainees via executive order, which was required by Section 1023 of the NDAA, and announced that periodic review boards would soon begin for 71 of the detainees.[147] Those periodic review board proceedings have subsequently commenced.[148] The Executive also submitted a report to congressional committees regarding implementation of the status determination process for wartime detainees required under Section 1024 of the act. Restrictions on Guantanamo detainee transfers contained in the 2012 NDAA and prior and subsequent legislative enactments are widely believed to have constrained executive efforts to transfer detainees to foreign custody.[149]

Prior to the enactment of the 2012 NDAA, it had been exceedingly rare for U.S. authorities to transfer a suspected terrorist from civilian to military custody. Section 1022 of the act, which generally requires foreign members of Al Qaeda or associated forces to be transferred (at least temporarily) to military custody, was seen by some observers as potentially having a profound impact on existing practice. When signing the 2012 NDAA into law, President Obama expressed opposition to the provision, and stated that his Administration would interpret and implement Section 1022 in a manner "that best preserves the same flexible approach that has served us so well for the past 3 years."[150] He further mentioned the provision's inclusion of authority for the President to waive its transfer requirements when he certified to Congress that it was in the national security interest of the United States to do so.

Section 1021 of the 2012 NDAA has continued to draw criticism on the basis that it permits detention without trial of certain individuals, possibly including U.S. citizens and others in the United States. A federal judge enjoined the detention of persons on the basis of providing support

---

[147] Rosenberg, *supra* footnote 58. Those to receive periodic review board hearings include 46 detainees who had been designated too dangerous to release but not prosecutable and 25 other detainees who were previously listed as candidates for trial by military commission or civilian court.

[148] *See* Department of Defense Press Release, *supra* footnote 59 (January 2014 announcement of completion of first periodic review board proceeding).

[149] Of the 166 detainees remaining at Guantanamo at the end of 2012, 56 were reportedly cleared by executive authorities for transfer pending negotiations with potential recipient countries, while another 30 detainees from Yemen could be repatriated if conditions there improve. Another 46 detainees were determined to be too dangerous to permit release, but are not being considered for military commission trial. Three of the detainees were convicted, charges were pending against seven others, and 24 detainees were under review for possible prosecution. *See* Government Accountability Office (GAO) Report 13-31, *Guantánamo Bay Detainees: Facilities and Factors for Consideration If Detainees Were Brought to the United States* 9 (November 2012). As of the date of this report, 17 more detainees were transferred from Guantanamo to foreign countries, reducing the detainee population to 149. *See* Andrei Scheinkman et al., "The Guantanamo Docket," NY TIMES, *at* http://projects nytimes.com/guantanamo.

[150] Presidential Signing Statement on 2012 NDAA, *supra* footnote 4.

---

to or associating with belligerent parties under one prong of the definition,[151] but the injunction was reversed on appeal due to lack of standing.[152]

Presidential Policy Directive 14

On February 28, 2012, the White House issued a presidential policy directive describing how it would implement Section 1022 and waiving the mandatory military detention requirement for several categories of persons.[153] The directive reiterates that Section 1022 will be implemented in a manner that enables the executive to largely preserve existing policies involving the handling of terrorist suspects,[154] and states that the FBI will continue to have "lead responsibility for investigations of terrorist acts or terrorist threats by individuals or groups within the United States, as well as for related intelligence collection activities within the United States."[155]

The directive declares that, acting pursuant to the statutory waiver authority provided under Section 1022, the President has waived application of the provision's military transfer requirements when

- a person in U.S. custody is a lawful permanent resident alien (i.e., green-card holder) who is arrested in the United States on the basis of conduct occurring inside the country;

- a person has been arrested by a federal agency in the United States on charges other than terrorism, unless he is subsequently charged with a terrorism offense and held in federal custody on such charges;

- a person is arrested by state or local law enforcement, pursuant to state or local authority,[156] and is thereafter transferred to federal custody;

- placing a foreign country's nationals or residents in U.S. military detention would impede counterterrorism cooperation, including on matters related to intelligence-sharing or assistance in the investigation or prosecution of suspected terrorists;

- a foreign government indicates that it will not extradite or otherwise transfer a person to the United States if he would be placed in military custody;

---

[151] Hedges v. Obama, 890 F. Supp. 2d 424 (S.D.N.Y. 2012). For a discussion of this case, see CRS Report R42337, *Detention of U.S. Persons as Enemy Belligerents*, by Jennifer K. Elsea.

[152] Hedges v. Obama, 724 F.3d 170 (2d Cir. 2013), *cert. denied*, 134 S. Ct. 1936 (2014).

[153] Presidential Policy Directive on Section 1022, *supra* footnote 5.

[154] The White House has stated that the "procedures are intended to ensure that the executive branch can continue to utilize all elements of national power—including military, intelligence, law enforcement, diplomatic, and economic tools—to effectively confront the threat posed by al-Qa'ida and its associated ... and will retain the flexibility to determine how best to apply those tools to the unique facts and circumstances we face in confronting this diverse and evolving threat." White House, *Fact Sheet: Procedures Implementing Section 1022 of the National Defense Authorization Act for Fiscal Year 2012* (February 28, 2012), *available at* http://www.whitehouse.gov/sites/default/files/ndaa_fact_sheet.pdf.

[155] Presidential Directive on Section 1022, *supra* footnote 5, at 9-10.

[156] The specification that the person is arrested "pursuant to state or local authority" suggests that this waiver may not be applicable when a state or local authority arrests a person for a violation of federal law.

- transferring a person to military custody could interfere with efforts to secure the person's cooperation or confession; or

- transferring a person to military custody could interfere with efforts to jointly prosecute the individual with others who are either not subject to military custody or whose prosecution in a federal or state court had already been determined to proceed.[157]

Some of these waivers apply to relatively definitive categories of individuals, such as the waiver covering legal permanent residents who have been arrested for domestic activities and the waiver applying to persons originally in state or local custody. The applicability of other waivers may depend upon more individualized determinations, including the impact that a person's military transfer would have upon ongoing law enforcement activities or foreign relations.

The directive then establishes procedures for determining whether a person coming into U.S. custody must be transferred to military detention as a "covered person" under Section 1022, which requires at least temporary detention of any non-citizen whose detention is authorized by the AUMF who is determined to be part of Al Qaeda or an associated force and to have participated in the planning or carrying out of an actual or attempted attack against the United States or its coalition partners. The procedures established by the directive do not apply when a suspect is initially taken into custody by DOD; in such circumstances, the relevant requirements of Section 1022 are interpreted as having "been satisfied ... regardless of the authorities under which the individual is captured, detained, or otherwise taken into custody."[158] The directive also interprets Section 1022 as being inapplicable to individuals while they are in the custody of state or local authorities or a foreign government. If a waiver applies, there is no need to make a final determination as to whether an individual is a "covered person" under Section 1022.

Before an individual may be transferred from a federal agency to military custody, the directive mandates that a multi-level review process must first occur. When a person is initially taken into federal law enforcement custody, and there is probable cause to believe the individual is a "covered person" under Section 1022, the arresting agency is required to notify the Attorney General. The Attorney General then makes a separate determination as to whether there is sufficient information to conclude that probable cause exists to believe that Section 1022 applies to the arrestee and that he is not exempted from the provision's application by waiver. If probable cause is found to be absent or an existing national security waiver is deemed applicable, no further action is necessary. Otherwise, the Attorney General, in coordination with senior national security officials, undertakes a closer review to determine whether Section 1022 applies to the arrestee.[159] If the Attorney General finds that there is clear and convincing evidence that the individual falls under the auspices of Section 1022 (a higher evidentiary standard than employed by the government when assessing whether someone may be detained as an enemy belligerent under the AUMF[160]) and no waiver applies, a final determination may then be made that the

---

[157] Presidential Directive on Section 1022, *supra* footnote 5, at 4-5.

[158] *Id.* at 3.

[159] *Id.* at 7. Appropriate agencies are required to assist in the collection of relevant information, including information pertaining to the citizenship or immigration status of the arrestee.

[160] In habeas litigation involving Guantanamo detainees, the executive branch has argued that it may satisfy its evidentiary burden in support of a person's detention when its factual claims are supported by a preponderance of evidence, and reliance on this standard has been upheld by the D.C. Circuit Court of Appeals. *See, e.g.,* Al Odah v. United States, 611 F.3d 8 (D.C. Cir. 2010) (upholding government's use of preponderance of evidence standard and specifically rejecting petitioner's argument that more rigorous clear and convincing evidence should be employed (continued...)

person is a "covered individual" with the concurrence of the Secretary of State, Secretary of Defense, Secretary of Homeland Security, and Director of National Intelligence.

The directive also delegates authority to the Attorney General to waive Section 1022 "on an individual, case-by-case basis" in the event that none of the blanket waivers applies. Such a waiver must be consistent with the statutory requirement that it be in the national security interest of the United States. A waiver can be issued without a final determination that an individual is a "covered person" under Section 1022. The directive lists several factors that the Attorney General is to take into account when determining whether such a waiver is warranted, including, *inter alia*,

- the legal and evidentiary strength of any criminal charges that may be brought against the person;

- the impact on intelligence collection which results from maintaining the person in law enforcement custody;

- "the risk associated with litigation concerning the legal authority to detain the individual pursuant to the 2001 AUMF"; and

- whether the prosecution of the individual in federal, state, or foreign court will otherwise best protect U.S. national security interests.[161]

Even assuming that a person is determined to be covered by Section 1022 and that no waiver will issue, his transfer to military custody may not be immediate. The directive specifies that, in the event that a person is determined to be covered by Section 1022, the federal law enforcement agency that took the arrestee into custody shall, in consultation with the Attorney General and Secretary of Defense, take steps to ensure that the transfer does not result in the interruption of an interrogation or compromise a national security investigation. The directive also provides that

> In no event may a Covered Person arrested in the United States or taken into custody ... [by a federal law enforcement agency] be transferred to military custody unless and until the Director of the FBI or his designee has determined such a transfer will not interrupt any ongoing interrogation, compromise any national security investigation, or interrupt any ongoing surveillance or intelligence gathering with regard to persons not already in the custody or control of the United States.... For these purposes, and to ensure that vital intelligence is not lost, an "interrogation" is not limited to a single interview session and extends until the interrogating agency or agencies determine that all necessary intelligence gathering efforts have been exhausted.[162]

The 2012 NDAA permits the President to waive Section 1022's military transfer requirements only when "such a waiver is in the national security interests of the United States."[163] Some observers have questioned whether all of the waivers issued or authorized under the directive are

---

(...continued)

instead), *cert. denied*, 131 S. Ct. 1812 (2011). The "preponderance of evidence standard" is generally interpreted to require that the evidence presented by both sides taken together makes the facts in question more likely true than not. *See* 29 AM. JUR. 2d Evid. §173. The "clear and convincing evidence" standard is somewhat more rigorous, requiring that a proposition is highly probable, but not requiring that the evidence negate all reasonable doubt. *Id.*

[161] *Id.* at 5.

[162] Presidential Directive on Section 1022, *supra* footnote 5, at 8-9.

[163] P.L. 112-81, §1022(a)(4).

consistent with this statutory requirement.[164] In any event, significant procedural barriers—including standing and political question concerns—may impede a legal suit challenging the propriety of a waiver, making judicial settlement of the matter appear unlikely. If Members of Congress disagree with the President's implementation of Section 1022, further legislative action may be considered.

The directive also provides that it is not intended to create any right or benefit enforceable by any party against the United States. The directive also asserts that a determination that clear and convincing evidence is lacking to subject a person to mandatory military detention is "without prejudice to the question of whether the individual may be subject to detention under the 2001 AUMF, as informed by the laws of war, and affirmed by Section 1021 of the NDAA."[165] Presumably, this is in part because the evidentiary standard employed by the Executive for assessing whether a person is subject to mandatory military detention under Section 1022 is heavier than the standard used by the executive when determining whether someone may be held as an enemy belligerent under the AUMF.[166]

FY2013 NDAA Detainee Provisions

The House version of the 2013 NDAA, H.R. 4310, was passed in May 2012. The Senate passed its version, S. 3254, as a substitute for the House bill on December 4, 2012. The House bill contained a number of restrictions on detainee transfers and requirements to submit detailed reports on such matters. The Senate bill contained extensions of certain restrictions from the 2012 NDAA. The bills addressed the issue of detention of U.S. persons inside the United States in different ways. The Obama Administration had threatened to veto both bills due to the restrictions on detainee transfers from Guantanamo, among other provisions.[167] The House and Senate met in conference to resolve differences between the competing bills, with the result that the detainee measures from the House version were largely adopted. The version of the 2013 NDAA that was reported from conference was subsequently approved by the House and Senate, and was presented to the President on December 30, 2012. The 2013 NDAA became law on January 2, 2013 (P.L. 112-239). The following paragraphs describe the act's provisions concerning wartime detention.

---

[164] *See, e.g.*, Jeremy Pelofsky and Laura MacInnis, *Obama Lays out Detention Rules for al Qaeda Suspects*, REUTERS (February 28, 2012) (quoting joint statement by Senators Ayotte, McCain, and Graham that some aspects of the directive "may contradict the intent" of the 2012 NDAA); Greg McNeal, *How President Obama Plans to Implement the NDAA's Military Custody Provisions*, FORBES ONLINE (February 29, 2012) (expressing skepticism that some of the waivers, including those applying to persons arrested by state or local authorities, implicate U.S. national security interests), *available at* http://www.forbes.com/sites/gregorymcneal/2012/02/29/how-president-obama-plans-to-implement-the-ndaas-military-custody-provisions/.

[165] Presidential Policy Directive on Section 1022, *supra* footnote 5, at 10.

[166] See text accompanying footnote 160, *supra*. Section 1022 detainees are also a limited subset of those detainable under Section 1021. Unlike those whose military detention is required, non-mandatory detainees need not have participated in an attack or attempted attack.

[167] *See* Statement of Administration Policy on H.R. 4310—National Defense Authorization Act for FY 2013, May 15, 2012, *available online at* http://www.whitehouse.gov/sites/default/files/omb/legislative/sap/112/saphr4310r_20120515.pdf; Statement of Administration Policy on S. 3254—National Defense Authorization Act for FY 2013, November 29, 2012, *available at* http://www.whitehouse.gov/sites/default/files/omb/legislative/sap/112/saps3254s_20121129.pdf.

Military trials for foreign terrorist suspects. The conference committee eliminated a provision adopted during House consideration of H.R. 4310[168] that would have required that a foreign national who "engages or has engaged in conduct constituting an offense relating to a terrorist attack" on a U.S. target, and who is subject to trial for the offense before a military commission, must be charged before a military commission rather than in federal court. An identical provision was found in the version of the 2012 NDAA originally passed by the House, but it was excised from the enacted version.[169]

Detainee transfers from Guantanamo. Many provisions in the 2012 NDAA affecting detainees at Guantanamo were scheduled to expire at the end of the fiscal year (though similar restrictions concerning the transfer of Guantanamo detainees are found in appropriations enactments in effect beyond that date). The 2013 NDAA effectively extends several of these provisions in the 2012 NDAA through FY2013, including the blanket funding bar on the transfer of Guantanamo detainees into the country (§1027);[170] the prohibition on using funds to construct or modify facilities to house these detainees in the United States (§1026); and certification requirements and restrictions on the transfer of Guantanamo detainees to foreign countries (§1028).[171] These three provisions were found in the versions of the bill passed by both the House and Senate. A provision from the House bill that was not retained in the enacted version of the 2013 NDAA would have barred any Guantanamo detainee who is "repatriated" to the former U.S. territories of Palau, Micronesia, or the Marshall Islands from traveling to the United States.[172]

Detainees held elsewhere abroad. The 2013 NDAA establishes new certification and congressional notification requirements relating to the transfer or release of non-U.S. or non-Afghan nationals held at the detention facility in Parwan, Afghanistan.[173] The 2013 NDAA also establishes reporting requirements relating to recidivism by former detainees in Afghanistan.[174] Specifically, it requires a report to be filed within 120 days describing the "estimated recidivism rates and the factors that appear to contribute to the recidivism of individuals formerly detained at the Detention Facility at Parwan, Afghanistan, who were transferred or released, including the estimated total number of individuals who have been recaptured on one or more occasion." This

---

[168] H.Amdt. 1105 to H.R. 4310, 112th Cong. (§1088 of the engrossed bill).

[169] See H.R. 1540 §1046 (as passed by the House of Representatives, 112th Cong.). For an analysis of the provision, see CRS Report R41920, *Detainee Provisions in the National Defense Authorization Bills*, by Jennifer K. Elsea and Michael John Garcia.

[170] The Senate version, as amended on the floor, would have expanded Section 1027 of the 2012 NDAA to all appropriated funds. S.Amdt. 3245.

[171] Section 1043 of the House bill would have changed the deadline for certifications or waivers of requirements from 30 to 90 days prior to the transfer. The version ultimately passed by Congress keeps the 30-day deadline from the 2012 NDAA. Other new requirements added by the House would have called for an "assessment of the likelihood that the individual to be transferred will engage in terrorist activity after the transfer takes place" and a "detailed summary... of the individual's history of associations with foreign terrorist organizations and the individual's record of cooperation while in the custody of or under the effective control of the Department of Defense." These requirements were omitted in conference.

[172] Section 1035 of H.R. 4310 (engrossed in the House) is substantially similar to H.R. 1540 Section 1043 (as passed by the House of Representatives, 112th Cong.), which was omitted during conference. For an analysis of the provision, see CRS Report R41920, *Detainee Provisions in the National Defense Authorization Bills*. H.R. 4310, as originally passed by the House, differed from the previous version in that it would deprive individuals only of rights named in Section 141 of the applicable Compact of Free Association.

[173] The measure appears to be a modified version of Section 1041 of the House-passed bill.

[174] P.L. 112-239 §1026.

is similar to Section 1042 of the House-passed bill, which had no analogous provision in the Senate version.[175]

The enacted version of the 2013 NDAA also retained a provision to require the Secretary of Defense to submit a report regarding the use of naval vessels to detain persons pursuant to the AUMF, and require congressional notification whenever such detention occurs.[176] This provision is presumably a response to the situation in 2011 when a Somali national was reportedly detained on a U.S. vessel for two months and interrogated by military and intelligence personnel before being brought into the United States to face criminal trial.[177]

Detention of persons in the United States. Despite the President's assurances that the Administration would not indefinitely detain Americans in the United States pursuant to the detention authorization in the 2012 NDAA, that provision has continued to draw criticism from some. The Senate adopted a measure that would have clarified that authorizations to use force are not to be construed to permit detention of U.S. citizens or lawful permanent residents in the United States unless Congress passes a law expressly authorizing such detention. This measure was eliminated from the bill reported out of conference.[178] An amendment to remove military detention as an optional "disposition under the law of war" for persons in the United States was proposed during floor debates in the House, but failed to garner sufficient votes for adoption.[179]

Instead, Section 1029 of the enacted version of the 2013 NDAA adopts a modified version of the House provision on habeas corpus rights.[180] It provides that nothing in the AUMF or 2012 NDAA is to be construed as denying "the availability of the writ of habeas corpus" or denying "any Constitutional rights in a court ordained or established by or under Article III of the Constitution" with respect to persons who are inside the United States who would be "entitled to the availability of such writ or to such rights in the absence of such laws." The original provision from the House-passed bill, as amended on the floor,[181] would have covered only persons who are lawfully present in the United States when detained pursuant to the AUMF. Under the floor amendment, the provision would also have required the President to notify Congress within 48 hours of the detention of such a person, and established a requirement that such persons be permitted to file for habeas corpus "not later than 30 days after the person is placed in military custody."

The 2013 NDAA does not contain substantive clarification of which U.S. persons are lawfully subject to detention under the AUMF. Sections from the House bill setting forth congressional

---

[175] Section 1042 of the House-passed version would have required an assessment of "recidivism rates and the factors that cause or contribute to the recidivism of individuals formerly detained at the Detention Facility at Parwan, Afghanistan, who are transferred or released, with particular emphasis on individuals transferred or released in connection with reconciliation efforts or peace negotiations"; and "a general rationale of the Commander, International Security Assistance Force, as to why such individuals were released."

[176] Section 1024 of H.R. 4310 (conference report) originated as Section 1040 of the House bill, which would have required notification within five days rather than 30.

[177] *See supra* footnote 20 and accompanying text.

[178] The measure, S.Amdt. 3018, is similar to S. 2003 and a companion bill, H.R. 3702, 112th Cong., entitled the Due Process Guarantee Act of 2011, and would have amended the Non-Detention Act, 18 U.S.C. §4001(a). For background of the Non-Detention Act and the legislation introduced to amend it, see CRS Report R42337, *Detention of U.S. Persons as Enemy Belligerents*, by Jennifer K. Elsea.

[179] H.Amdt. 1127.

[180] Section 1033 of H.R. 4310 (engrossed in the House, 112th Cong.).

[181] H.Amdt. 1126.

---

findings with respect to detention authority under the AUMF and 2012 NDAA and with respect to habeas corpus were omitted from the final version. Consequently, ambiguity with respect to who can be lawfully detained in the United States appears to have been preserved, but the enacted version of the 2013 NDAA provides reassurance that access to a court to petition for habeas corpus will remain available to those who are detained in the United States pursuant to the AUMF.

FY2014 NDAA Detainee Provisions

The House of Representatives passed a version of the National Defense Authorization Act for FY2014, H.R. 1960, on June 14, 2013. The Senate Armed Services Committee ordered its version of the 2014 NDAA, S. 1197, to be favorably reported out of committee on June 20, 2013.[182] On December 9, 2013, leaders on the House and Senate Armed Services Committees announced an agreement on a new defense authorization bill for FY2014, H.R. 3304, which was intended to resolve some of the key differences between the earlier House and Senate proposals.[183] One of those differences had been the bills' approaches to enemy belligerents housed at Guantanamo. House-passed H.R. 1960 would have preserved (and in some ways strengthened) the existing limitations on the transfer of Guantanamo detainees to the United States or to the custody of foreign governments. In contrast, S. 1197 would have relaxed restrictions on transfers to foreign countries, and would have permitted detainees to be brought to the United States for continued detention and possible trial. H.R. 3304 represented a compromise between these approaches—extending the current blanket prohibition on transferring Guantanamo detainees to the United States through the end of 2014, but allowing the Executive greater flexibility in determining whether to transfer detainees to foreign custody. H.R. 3304 was thereafter passed by Congress and presented to the President, and the bill became law on December 26, 2013.

The enacted version of the 2014 NDAA contains provisions addressing the following detention matters:

Transfer of Guantanamo detainees to the United States. Like the version of the 2014 NDAA initially passed by the House, the enacted version of the 2014 NDAA contains an absolute bar on the transfer of Guantanamo detainees into the United States for any purpose, and also prohibits the building or modifying of facilities in the United States to house such detainees. Both prohibitions expire at the end of 2014.[184] Similar to House-passed H.R. 1960, the enacted version of the 2014 NDAA requires a report to be submitted to Congress concerning the legal rights that might attach to detainees if they are transferred to the United States.[185]

Transfer of Guantanamo detainees to foreign countries. As previously discussed, in recent years appropriations and defense authorization enactments have permitted Guantanamo detainees to be transferred to foreign countries only when the Executive certifies to Congress that stringent criteria have been satisfied. The enacted version of the 2014 NDAA relaxes these restrictions in a

---

[182] S.Rept. 113-44.

[183] Senate Committee on Armed Services, Press Release, December 9, 2013, *available at* http://www.armed-services.senate.gov/imo/media/doc/Press%20release.pdf.

[184] 2014 NDAA, P.L. 113-66, §§1033-1034.

[185] *Id.* at §1039. An unclassified copy of this report, dated May 14, 2014, may be viewed at https://www.documentcloud.org/documents/1160074-5-14-14-kadzik-to-pjl-re-fy14-ndaa.html.

manner closely resembling that found in S. 1197.[186] Section 1035 of the enacted 2014 NDAA established permanent restrictions on detainee transfers, in contrast to earlier appropriations and defense authorization enactments which included restrictions applicable for specified periods (e.g., until the end of a given year or for the duration of a fiscal year). It permits detainee transfers under two specified circumstances: (1) when a detainee has been ordered released by a competent U.S. court or the detainee has been assessed by a Periodic Review Board as no longer posing a threat to the United States; (2) the Secretary of Defense determines that the transfer is in the U.S. national security interest and that actions have been or will be taken to substantially mitigate the risk of recidivism.[187]

The provision requires the Secretary to consider several factors in making such determinations, but does not require written certification to Congress that identified goals have been achieved as a prerequisite to executing a transfer. The Secretary is required, however, to provide the relevant congressional committee with notice at least 30 days in advance before transferring a Guantanamo detainee to a foreign country. As noted *infra*,[188] the executive branch's non-compliance with this notification requirement when effectuating the transfer of five Taliban members from Guantanamo in exchange for the release of U.S. Sgt. Bowe Bergdahl may inform future congressional deliberations upon the nature of statutory restrictions on detainee transfers.[189]

Like House-passed H.R. 1960, the final version of the 2014 NDAA requires the Executive to report to Congress regarding the capability of Yemen to detain, rehabilitate, or prosecute detainees who might be transferred there.[190] Unlike the earlier House bill, however, the enacted legislation does not statutorily bar the transfer of any detainee to Yemen through 2014.[191]

Parwan detainees. Like the original House version, the enacted 2014 NDAA contains a requirement that the Executive provide information regarding persons held by U.S. forces at the detention facility in Parwan, Afghanistan, who have been deemed to constitute an enduring threat

---

[186] *Id.* at §1035. In a statement issued following the signing of the 2014 NDAA, the White House characterized the act's relaxation of transfer restrictions as an "improvement" over prior law, but nonetheless viewed its restrictions as still too stringent:

> Section 1035 does not, however, eliminate all of the unwarranted limitations on foreign transfers and, in certain circumstances, would violate constitutional separation of powers principles. The executive branch must have the flexibility, among other things, to act swiftly in conducting negotiations with foreign countries regarding the circumstances of detainee transfers. Of course, even in the absence of any statutory restrictions, my Administration would transfer a detainee only if the threat the detainee may pose can be sufficiently mitigated and only when consistent with our humane treatment policy. Section 1035 nevertheless represents an improvement over current law and is a welcome step toward closing the facility.

White House Press Release, *Statement by the President on H.R. 3304*, December 26, 2013, *available at* http://www.whitehouse.gov/the-press-office/2013/12/26/statement-president-hr-3304.

[187] 2014 NDAA, P.L. 113-66, §1035. *See also* House Committee on Armed Services, Committee Print 2, Legislative Text and Joint Explanatory Statement to Accompany the National Defense Authorization Act for FY2014 (December 2013), at 633.

[188] *See infra* at "Detainee Provisions in FY2015 Defense Authorization Bills."

[189] *See generally* CRS Legal Sidebar WSLG956, Will the Guantanamo Bay Prisoner Exchange Influence Congress's Consideration of the Defense Authorization Bill?, by Michael John Garcia.

[190] 2014 NDAA, P.L. 113-66, §1038.

[191] H.R. 3304, 113th Cong., §1040D.

to the United States.[192] But whereas the original House proposal would have required an unclassified summary to be made publicly available,[193] the enacted version instead requires DOD to submit a classified report to the Armed Forces Committees and for it to assess whether any information contained in the report may be made public.

Military commissions. Like the initial House and Senate proposals, the enacted version of the 2014 NDAA clarifies procedures for the use of alternate members on military commissions employed to try some detainees for war crimes.[194] The 2014 NDAA also includes a provision similar to one found in House-passed H.R. 1960 requiring that the chief defense counsel in military commissions have the same rank as the chief prosecutor. However, the enacted version allows this requirement to be waived in some circumstances (and followed by a report to Congress), and additionally instructs DOD to issue guidance for the equitable allocation of resources and support to the prosecution and defense in military commission proceedings.

Detention of persons in the United States. As result of a floor amendment,[195] the initial House-passed bill contained a provision similar to that in the 2013 NDAA which stated that those apprehended pursuant to the AUMF in the United States were not barred from seeking habeas relief, except that this provision would have applied only to U.S. citizens (§1040B(a)). The section further provided that in cases where U.S. citizens apprehended within the United States petition for habeas corpus, the "government shall have the burden of proving by clear and convincing evidence that such citizen is an unprivileged enemy belligerent and there shall be no presumption that any evidence presented by the government as justification for the apprehension and subsequent detention is accurate and authentic" (§1040B(b)). This evidentiary standard appears to be higher than that which the courts of the D.C. Circuit have applied to cases involving Guantanamo detainees. In those cases, the government need only prove detention is lawful by a preponderance of the evidence, and there is a presumption that official government records submitted as evidence are authentic.[196] The provision was not included in the final enactment, which does not expressly address the detention of persons in the United States.

Detainee Provisions in FY2015 Defense Authorization Bills

As part of its consideration of defense authorization bills for the 2015 fiscal year, Congress is once again contemplating U.S. wartime detention policy in the conflict with Al Qaeda, particularly as it relates to the detention of suspected enemy belligerents at the Guantanamo detention facility. The House passed its version of the 2015 National Defense Authorization Act (2015 NDAA), H.R. 4435, on May 22, 2014. It would extend existing limitations on the transfer of Guantanamo detainees to the United States through 2015, and would not alter those permanent laws governing the transfer of detainees to the custody of foreign governments. In contrast, the version of the 2015 NDAA reported out of the Senate Armed Services Committee, S. 2410, would significantly alter current restrictions on the transfer of Guantanamo detainees into the United States, and potentially enable the Executive to transfer most of the current detainee population

---

[192] 2014 NDAA, P.L. 113-66, §1036.

[193] H.R. 3304, 113th Cong., §1035.

[194] 2014 NDAA, P.L. 113-66, §1031.

[195] H.Amdt. 150.

[196] *See supra* footnote 160; CRS Report R41156, *Judicial Activity Concerning Enemy Combatant Detainees: Major Court Rulings*, by Jennifer K. Elsea and Michael John Garcia.

into the country for continued detention or trial. S. 2410, as reported, would also modify current law by barring the transfer of detainees to Yemen for the duration of 2015.

Shortly after H.R. 4435 was passed by the House and S. 2410 was ordered reported by the Senate Armed Services Committee, the United States transferred five Taliban detainees from Guantanamo as part of an exchange to effectuate the release of U.S. Sgt. Bowe Bergdahl, who had been held captive by Taliban-affiliated forces for several years. In completing this prisoner exchange, the Executive did not comply with notification requirements contained in Section 1035 of the 2014 NDAA, which require it to notify Congress at least 30 days before a detainee transfer occurs. The Executive has asserted that Section 1035 should not be interpreted to apply to the exchange, as it would have interfered with the President's attempt to rescue a U.S. soldier and potentially raise constitutional concerns.[197] It seems likely that the recent prisoner exchange, along with the Executive's interpretation of the scope of current statutory restrictions on Guantanamo detainee transfers, will inform congressional deliberations on defense authorization legislation for FY2015.

The following topics concerning wartime detention are addressed by either the House-passed or Senate version of the 2015 NDAA, or by both bills.

Transfer of Guantanamo detainees to the United States. The House-passed version of the 2015 NDAA would extend the bar on the transfer of Guantanamo detainees into the United States for any purpose,[198] and also continue the prohibition on building or modifying of facilities in the United States to house such detainees.[199] Both restrictions would last through December 31, 2015.

The Senate version of the 2015 NDAA reported out of committee, in contrast, would potentially enable the executive branch to facilitate the closure of the Guantanamo detention facility, including by permitting the transfer of detainees into the United States for continued detention or trial.[200] The bill would generally extend the current prohibition on the transfer or release of detainees into the United States through FY2015.[201] However, this prohibition would be altered in the event that the Secretary of Defense submits a plan to close the Guantanamo detention facility to appropriate congressional committees. The bill provides for fast-track consideration of a joint resolution of disapproval of the submitted plan. If a joint resolution of disapproval was not enacted into law, DOD would be permitted to transfer persons from Guantanamo into the United States for continued wartime detention and/or trial.[202] Prior to a transfer occurring, the Secretary of Defense would be required to determine that the transfer was in U.S. security interests and that sufficient actions had or would be taken to reduce any public safety risks posed by the transfer.[203] Notification to Congress would be required not later than 30 days before the proposed transfer.[204] The Senate bill would prohibit transferred detainees from subsequently being released within the United States, limit judicial review of matters concerning transferred detainees' continued

---

[197] For further discussion, see CRS Legal Sidebar WSLG956, *Will the Guantanamo Bay Prisoner Exchange Influence Congress's Consideration of the Defense Authorization Bill?*, by Michael John Garcia.

[198] H.R. 4435, §1033.

[199] *Id.* §1032.

[200] S. 2410, §1031.

[201] *Id.* §1031(a).

[202] *Id.* §1031(b), (g).

[203] *Id.* §1031(b).

[204] *Id.* §1031(c).

detention, and bar transferred detainees from applying for asylum or admission into the United States pursuant to the nation's immigration laws.[205]

The Senate bill contains a separate exception to the current restrictions on the transfer of detainees into the United States. It would permit the temporary transfer of a detainee into the United States for purposes of medical treatment in limited circumstances, subject to conditions intended to ensure that a transferred detainee would not obtain any rights or benefits under U.S. immigration laws or other federal statutes.[206] Significantly, this exception is not tied to the provision described in the preceding paragraph, which would allow the transfer of detainees into the country for continued detention and trial only if specific requirements were satisfied.

Construction of facilities at Guantanamo. The Senate bill would also bar the use of funds made available for FY2015 from being used to construct new facilities at Guantanamo, except when the Secretary of Defense certifies that such facilities have enduring military value separate from serving "a high value detention mission."[207] This prohibition does not apply to the use of funds to correct deficiencies that are threatening to health and safety.

Transfer of Guantanamo detainees to foreign countries. The House-passed version of the NDAA would not modify those permanent laws governing the transfer of detainees to the custody of foreign governments. The Senate bill, as reported out of committee, would bar the use of DOD funds to transfer or release any Guantanamo detainee to Yemen for the duration through December 31, 2015. It would also require the Secretary of Defense and Secretary of State to jointly submit a report to specified congressional committees regarding actions taken or planned to be taken to facilitate the transfer of Guantanamo detainees to foreign countries in the future.[208]

Author Contact Information

Jennifer K. Elsea
Legislative Attorney
jelsea@crs.loc.gov, 7-5466

Michael John Garcia
Legislative Attorney
mgarcia@crs.loc.gov, 7-3873

---

[205] *Id.* §1031(d)-(f).

[206] *Id.* §1033.

[207] *Id.* at §2806.

[208] *Id.* at §1032.

www.ingramcontent.com/pod-product-compliance
Lightning Source LLC
Chambersburg PA
CBHW052018280526

45793CB00005B/1026